T0334776

WONDERSTRUCK

Wonderstruck

HOW WONDER AND AWE SHAPE THE WAY WE THINK

HELEN DE CRUZ

PRINCETON UNIVERSITY PRESS
PRINCETON & OXFORD

Published by Princeton University Press
41 William Street, Princeton, New Jersey 08540
99 Banbury Road, Oxford OX2 6JX

press.princeton.edu

Library of Congress Cataloging-in-Publication Data

Names: De Cruz, Helen, 1978– author.
Title: Wonderstruck : how wonder and awe shape the way we think / Helen De Cruz.
Description: Princeton : Princeton University Press, [2024] | Includes bibliographical references and index.
Identifiers: LCCN 2023028348 (print) | LCCN 2023028349 (ebook) | ISBN 9780691232126 (hardback) | ISBN 9780691232171 (ebook)
Subjects: LCSH: Wonder (Philosophy) | BISAC: PHILOSOPHY / Epistemology | SCIENCE / Natural History
Classification: LCC B105.W65 D42 2024 (print) | LCC B105.W65 (ebook) | DDC 128—dc23/eng/20231004
LC record available at https://lccn.loc.gov/2023028348
LC ebook record available at https://lccn.loc.gov/2023028349

British Library Cataloging-in-Publication Data is available

Editorial: Rob Tempio and Chloe Coy
Production Editorial: Ali Parrington
Jacket Design: Heather Hansen
Production: Erin Suydam
Publicity: Maria Whelan

Jacket image: *Comet Donati*, 1858. Science History Images / Alamy Stock Photo

This book has been composed in Arno

Printed on acid-free paper. ∞

Printed in the United States of America

10 9 8 7 6 5 4 3 2 1

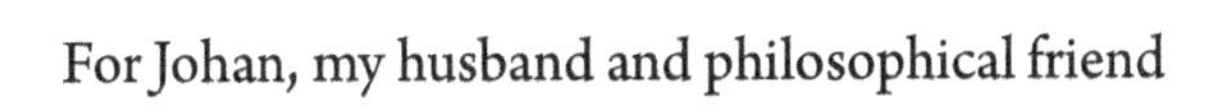
For Johan, my husband and philosophical friend

CONTENTS

ILLUSTRATIONS

WONDERSTRUCK

1

Freedom to Wonder

Amateur Astronomy

“Come on, everyone out of the house!” My neighbor called his wife and children to come out and gaze at the sky. We all stood in that quiet suburban street in Saint Louis, Missouri, watching for a while, waiting for the blood moon to make a furtive appearance from behind a persistent veil of clouds. Finally, near midnight, we beheld the wine-red disc. My daughter asked, "So, this is a total lunar eclipse? If it's total, why can I still see the moon?" (The reason is that some sunlight is still hitting it.)

Blood moons are spectacular, but they are by no means extraordinary. Total lunar eclipses can be seen every few years from any given location. It's easy to become jaded about them. While others hauled dusty amateur telescopes out of attics and spread out blankets for midnight picnics to enjoy the blood moon that spring night, science communicator Neil deGrasse Tyson commented, "Lunar eclipses are so un-spectacular that if nobody told you what was happening to the Moon you'd probably not notice at all."[1] There is, however, no objective fact of the matter of how spectacular or unspectacular lunar eclipses are. How we react to them is up to us. We wonder at something outside of us (usually), but wonder comes from within.

The moon has struck wonder into people across the world. It features in fairytales, myths, and dreams, it is the abode of lost lovers and irresistible pull for werewolves. It was the object of intense intellectual pursuit, with people from sub-Saharan Africa (Dogon), Warring States China, and ancient Greece seeking to predict lunar eclipses. Its phases seem fickle, yet are predictable to patient eyes. The lunar calendar of Abri Blanchard, dated to about thirty-two thousand years ago, is a piece of antler incised with some seventy morphologically distinct notches that map out the successive phases of the moon, their serpentine trajectory reflecting the actual position of the spring moon in the sky of the Dordogne region (France) upon setting.[2] We do not know much about the Pleistocene hunter-gatherers who crafted this calendar, but they—very much like us today—looked up in wonder at the night sky.

If you live in an urban area with significant light pollution, as in most of the industrialized world, the moon is one of the main astronomical features you can still observe with the naked eye. Our cities are swathed in the constant glow of artificial light, which means that many of us have never beheld the Milky Way, our home galaxy. So, when you look up at the night sky, it is not quite the same as what the philosophers we'll encounter in this book—Fontenelle, Kant, and others—saw whenever they looked up on a clear night. The black expanse they witnessed was a rich tapestry tinged with subtle hues of purples, pinks, and rose madder, strewn with thousands of stars of various sizes. It is hard to imagine that so many people in the past thought of these stars as fixed on a celestial orb, and saw their whole universe as a tight ball of neatly nested spheres, the fixed stars precious but ultimately tractable jewels.

Today we know that the universe is vast. That vastness, conceptually, can be a source of awe and wonder. On July 11, 2022, NASA unveiled infrared imagery made by the Webb telescope of galaxies nearly thirteen billion light years away—thirteen billion years ago, that is, when the universe was very young.[3] The pictures show a rich collection of very bright little discs, each of them a nascent galaxy consisting of billions of stars, the images covering in total that part of the field of vision of a human observer focusing on a grain of sand held at arm's length. The most distant galaxies recede from us at a pace that exceeds the speed of light. The further away a galaxy is, the faster it appears to travel from us (this is known as Hubble–Lemaître's law).[4]

In a quiet, reflective state of mind that gives you the suppleness and scope you need to take a step back, you will probably have experienced moments of awe and wonder. You don't even need the night sky—something small and mundane such as an insect scurrying up a blade of grass or an autumn leaf half-submerged in a frozen puddle is sufficient. The experience of wonder belongs to all of us, not just to children, scientists, or philosophers. Descartes called wonder the first of the passions, the passion that precedes judgment. The moment we wonder at some object or event, we do not (yet) evaluate it as positive or negative. We do not contemplate whether the thing we wonder at will be helpful or harmful. To understand awe and wonder is to appreciate an important and enduring aspect of being human.

In this book, I will treat awe and wonder as distinct, but psychologically related emotions. To get us on the same page, here are some provisional working definitions which will be further fleshed out and motivated in the next two chapters:

> *Awe* is the emotion we sense when we perceive or conceptualize vastness, combined with a need for cognitive accommodation. Cognitive accommodation means we want to make space in our minds for this vast thing. Vastness can be physical (sheer size) or conceptual (e.g., complexity). Exemplars of things we can be in awe of include the night sky, a monumental, high building such as a temple or pyramid, a great and encompassing theory, superlative feats by a living being, and an astonishing mathematical result.
>
> *Wonder* is the emotion that arises from a glimpse at the unknown terrain which lies just beyond the fringes of our current understanding. Like awe, it prompts a need for cognitive accommodation, but it does not necessarily have the dimension of vastness. Examples of elicitors include the intricacy of an insect seen under a microscope, an unusual fossil or strangely shaped crystal, and an unexpected astronomical event.

My motivation for treating awe and wonder together is the historical close connection between them in Western theorizing.

Words such as the ancient Greek *thauma* and the medieval *admiratio* encompass both awe and wonder. As we'll see in chapter 3, contemporary psychologists also treat them as related.

Awe and wonder share two salient features. First, they are *epistemic emotions*, emotions that motivate us to explore our environment and learn more about it.[5] These emotions are concerned with obtaining knowledge and related mental states.[6] Epistemic emotions include curiosity, doubt, wonder, awe, and surprise. While scientists experience such emotions often, they occur in many domains of human life: for example, in gossip about extramarital affairs, when we want to know what happens in a novel, and when we're puzzling out a sudoku grid. Nonhuman animals can also feel curiosity at a new feature of their environment. Your cat might find a novel way into the kitchen pantry. Though it sometimes proves fatal to cats, curiosity is very often advantageous.

Some epistemic feelings let us know that we know. These include the feeling of knowing, the feeling of certainty, and the feeling of correctness. For example, you feel sure that "1666" is the answer to the question, "When did the Great Fire of London occur?" Feeling that you know, even that you are sure, is not infallible. We can be mistaken in those feelings. Other epistemic feelings alert our attention to what we do not yet know. Curiosity, awe, and wonder fall into this category. As with the feelings of knowing, we can ask whether feelings of not-yet-knowing are necessarily right. It does seem that if you wonder at something, there is something that prompted you to wonder. This feeling alerts you to the fact that your current body of knowledge—the schemas, heuristics, and other information you use—did not prepare you for the thing you wonder at. As such, wonder is a useful emotion, because it points to gaps in what you thought you knew. For example, many of my

American friends express wonder when I (as a Belgian) tell them there are several types of Belgian waffles, and that the concept of Belgian waffle doesn't exist in Belgium. A whole world of waffles opens up in their imagination, a panoply of unknown culinary adventures and delights.

Second, awe and wonder are *self-transcendent emotions*: they help us move away from a focus on ourselves and our own concerns. They help us to open ourselves up to our environment. Self-transcendent emotions are primarily social, though they can also be directed at our natural world, making us aware of its beauty and perhaps also its fragility. They include compassion, love, and gratitude.[7]

The epistemic and self-transcendent aspects of awe and wonder work together: to learn more about the world and ourselves, we need to defamiliarize ourselves. We need to think outside of existing schemas and heuristics. For example, when we learn that plants communicate with each other using chemical signals, this challenges our notion that plants are just sessile things we can put in flowerbeds or cut down as we see fit. Awe and wonder offer us the emotional space to be able to do this: either to see something for the first time, or to see something *as if* for the first time, and to accept the immensity and wondrousness of it, without trying to categorize it or box it in. The ability to do this is crucial. It governs our pursuits of knowledge. As we'll see, it also plays a role in our ethical lives.

Culture in Service of Human Needs

Like other emotions, awe and wonder are part of our cultural environment. While they do have an evolutionary basis (see chapter 3), they are culturally scaffolded. For this reason, it will be useful to briefly lay out here my overall picture of human culture and its relationship to our nature as biological and cultural creatures.

For as long as I can remember, I've been fascinated by domains of higher cognition and culture, such as the arts, the sciences, mathematics, and theology. I grew up in the blue-collar household of an immigrant father who was a bricklayer and a mother who was a homemaker. Money was often tight. Life often felt like a struggle to get to the end of the month, repeated from one month to the next. What would happen if the car broke down, or did not pass inspection? What would happen if my father was (as could happen seasonally) out of work? In spite of this, we enjoyed the deeper pursuits of human life, such as literature, music, and nature. My father had a darkroom for black-and-white photography. My mother collected stamps with exotic birds from across the world. My sister had a passion for STEM (and would eventually earn a PhD in physics) and had various chemistry kits to do her own experiments at home. And I had so many books that they did not fit in my rickety bookcase, but had to be placed in stacks on the floor. I also read most books in the local village library. Taking us beyond the pure economic calculus of putting food on the table each month, these things made our lives joyful, meaningful, and worthwhile. I loved visiting art and science museums, and would spend long afternoons marveling at their exhibits. As I looked at landscapes by European masters, steam engines, African masks, Persian astrolabes, I would wonder, "Why do we make this stuff?" The sheer profligacy of human culture has always struck me. Consequently, I have spent a large part of my academic career trying to understand why humans engage in philosophy, religious reflection, mathematics, art, and science. What drives mathematicians to try to prove the Collatz conjecture? What motivates theologians to come up with obscure and complicated pictures of how the persons of the Trinity relate in Christianity or of avataric incarnation in Hinduism? What pushes scientists to understand the structure of reality, without even knowing whether their endeavors will succeed or bear any practical fruit?

We spend what seem on the face of it outlandish amounts of time and energy on these pursuits, which appear to be inessential in keeping us alive in the struggle for survival and reproduction. Why make life even more complicated than it already is? Policy makers and pundits have, for decades, been singing the same tune: the humanities, including literature, art, music, and philosophy, are a waste of time. They tell us to focus on useful fields that will help us address more tangible problems, such as carbon capture to combat climate change. This attitude is built on philosophically shaky grounds: namely, that to tackle problems such as climate change, political polarization, warfare, inequality, or pandemics we don't need to change our way of life or our outlook at all; it suffices simply to apply a technological fix. As a result of this consensus, funding for the humanities has been slashed in most wealthy countries.[8] And yet, even in times and places where humans did not have access to such things as industrial crop farming (yielding a steady stream of food), modern medicine (yielding increased life expectancy across the world), and fossil-fuel powered technology, we enjoyed the excesses. Art, philosophy, and religion lay serious claims to being true human universals.[9] We find them in societies with widely diverging technologies, social organization, and means of subsistence. If humans across times and cultures have found these pursuits worthwhile, we should ask why this is so. The scarcity narrative that surrounds us tells us that there is no more money to make art, philosophy, and other fine culture accessible to everyone. Yet, humans who were and are much worse off, in material terms,[10] than industrialized Westerners still spend significant time and energy on these pursuits.

The philosopher Daniel Dennett was struck by these profligacies of human culture, specifically religion, with its feasts and festivals, temples, dances, the deep reflection on sacred texts, and seemingly arbitrary constraints on what to eat and what to wear.[11] He insists, and I agree, that this apparent "wastefulness" requires an explanation. If we observed the apparent excesses of human culture in any other species, we would try to account for their existence in biological terms. Indeed, in evolutionary biology we can see explanations for why, for example, flowers have vivid colors, bird song is elaborate, and why peacocks have lush, cumbersome tails with bold eye-spots that glisten green and purple. Dennett has an evolutionary explanation for religion: he likens our brains to those of hapless ants infested with the lancet fluke parasite. Just as the parasite commandeers the ant to climb up a blade of grass to increase its chance of ending up in a ruminant's stomach (and hence complete the parasite's reproductive cycle), religious ideas infest our brains, replicating themselves at our expense.

While I agree with Dennett that religions and other higher pursuits are remarkable and require an explanation, I disagree that we can explain them as self-interested cultural phenomena. As anthropologist Dan Sperber notes, you cannot explain culture with culture.[12] Rather, my guiding assumption in this book is that culture serves human needs and interests generated by body and mind. The products of our cultures are fitted to respond to these needs and interests, in ways that nurture and sustain us. For example, we live in artifacts (such as houses) that we build to protect us from the elements. This is not to say that human culture always comes up with optimal solutions. It also allows for the possibility of maladaptive cultural practices, or for culture to be used to manipulate, exploit, or deceive others, such as in the case of slavery as an institution in many cultures.

Nevertheless, any approach to human culture should put the biological organisms that came up with it, and that live and breathe it, at its center.

Many contemporary authors who study the origins and spread of human cultures have likewise proposed that cultures respond to human needs. For example, we have accounts of the evolution and function of religion, technology, and culture more generally.[13] Human needs are broader than the ones we might narrowly think of in an evolutionary context. We might be tempted, along with policy makers and pundits, to think that to survive simply means having food and shelter, and to reproduce is to have offspring that survive. When we apply this lens to our social world, we neglect the importance of play, leisure, self-expression, and free exploration. Already in the 1950s, the anthropologist Leslie White (1900–1975) proposed that any scientific study of culture needs to ground itself in our nature as biological organisms. However, he denied that we can trace back all cultural achievements to biological needs, narrowly conceived. The purpose of culture is to serve our needs, but, as he recognized, our needs are not only material. We have

> inner, psychic, social, and "spiritual" needs that can be fed and nourished without drawing upon the external world at all. Man needs courage, comfort, consolation, confidence, companionship, a feeling of consequence in the scheme of things that life is worthwhile, and some assurance of success. It is the business of culture to serve these needs of the "spirit" as well as the needs of the body.[14]

White observed that human lives are a struggle, marred by pain, suffering, loneliness, and frustration. Here is where culture serves us:

> Mythologies flatter, encourage, and reassure man. By means of magic and ritual he can capture the illusion of power and control over things and events: he can "control" the weather, cure disease, foresee the future, increase his food supply, overcome his enemies. Cosmologies give him answers to all fundamental questions, of life and death and the nature of all things.[15]

Thus, White aimed to provide an overarching, functionalist explanation of three aspects of human culture which have long intrigued anthropologists: magic, religion, and science. They are three kinds of cultural practices that attempt to harness power and control over our environment.

In a similar vein, the pragmatist philosopher and early psychologist William James (1842–1910) emphasized the importance of a broad range of spiritual and cognitive needs for human flourishing. To recognize this is not antithetical to an evolutionary approach to culture; it is an integral part of it. James critiqued Herbert Spencer's evolutionary view of the mind.[16] The first edition of Spencer's *Principles of Psychology* was published before Charles Darwin's landmark *Origin of Species*.[17] It attempted to apply evolutionary principles to psychology. Spencer argued that our minds are fine-tuned through evolution to help us survive and reproduce. James criticized Spencer: if cognition is only about an animal's representation of the environment (to help it survive and reproduce), then what of "all sentiments, all aesthetic impulses, all religious emotions and personal affections?"[18] It seems that something essential is being left out, "simply because, to common sense, survival is only one out of many interests."[19] Attempts to reduce emotions and human needs to a function of biology don't do justice to the full scope of what our interests might be. James specifies these interests as

> all that makes survival worth securing. The social affections, all the various forms of play, the thrilling intimations of art, the delights of philosophic contemplation, the rest of religious emotion, the joy of moral self-approbation, the charm of fancy and of wit—some or all of these are absolutely required to make the notion of mere existence tolerable.[20]

Here, James makes important claims. We value "the story-teller, the musician, the theologian, the actor." People in these professions "have never lacked means of support, however helpless they might individually have been to conform with those outward relations which we know as the powers of nature."[21] James invokes a notion crucial in American pragmatism, namely the interconnectedness of the individual within a broader society: the interests of our fellow human beings are part of our environment. Even if theologians, philosophers, and scientists are not well adapted to survive in a hypothetical (never actual) state of nature, they are able to survive if they can respond to the wants of their social groups.

Our social groups, I will argue, have a continued thirst for the wondrous and the awe-inspiring. My central thesis throughout this book is that awe and wonder are emotions that we harness by means of cultural practices, that we nurture deliberately, and that are part of a positive feedback loop. Because we feel awe and wonder, we come up with ideas and inventions in the sciences, arts, and other domains of human cultures. Those ideas in turn become objects of awe and wonder, and push us to ever further heights. I regard awe and wonder as instrumental to our overall engagement with the world. They help us to learn more, they keep our thirst for knowledge alive, and they push us to seek that knowledge outside of our pre-existing ways of thinking.

What This Book Is About: Awe and Wonder as Firstness

The view of awe and wonder I develop in this book is inspired by, and has significant resonances with Descartes's view of the passions, as outlined in his *Passions of the Soul* (1649). A more detailed discussion of Descartes's ideas will follow in the next chapter, but I will here briefly review why I find them fruitful. It's important to do so, as Descartes and Cartesianism have a bad rap in psychology. For example, the neuroscientist Antonio Damasio titled one of his books *Descartes' Error*, emblematic of the contempt some neuroscientists express for the early modern French philosopher. Damasio does not provide a detailed dismantling of Descartes's views and explanation as to why they might be erroneous, but instead treats him as a stock figure and caricature of mind–body dualism. According to Damasio, Descartes does not acknowledge the role of emotions in informing our decision making, and he sees human beings as fragmented into two independent substances, body and soul, without a clear idea of how these work together. This conception of him is mistaken, as Deborah Brown and others have demonstrated.[22] Contrary to popular imagination, Descartes does have a unified picture of how soul and body work together, and the passions play a crucial role in this. What Descartes called passions are more or less what we call emotions. They are crucial instruments that inform the soul about the world.[23]

Descartes argued that we cannot be misled about our passions in the way that our perceptions are sometimes tricked by illusions:

> We cannot be misled in the same way regarding the passions, in that they are so close and so internal to our soul that it

> cannot possibly feel them unless they are truly as it feels them to be [. . . ;] we cannot feel sad, or moved by any other passion, unless the soul truly has this passion within it.[24]

Descartes acknowledges the importance of the passions in our overall happiness and well-being in his final paragraph:

> *It is on the passions alone that all the good and evil of this life depends*
>
> For the rest, the soul can have pleasures of its own. But the pleasures common to it and the body depend entirely on the passions, so that persons whom the passions can move most deeply are capable of enjoying the sweetest pleasures of this life. It is true that they may also experience the most bitterness when they do not know how to put these passions to good use and when fortune works against them. But the chief use of wisdom lies in its teaching us to be masters of our passions and to control them with such skill that the evils which they cause are quite bearable, and even become a source of joy.[25]

According to Descartes, the passions are crucial for our lives, because they inform us about our environment. However, we are not doomed to be their slaves. Through training and attentiveness, we can attune our passions so they can do the work that we want them to do. This will help us to live in harmony with our social and natural environment, and achieve the sweetest pleasures that life has to offer.

Thus, while Descartes thinks that our passions are not voluntary (they happen to us; in this he is in line with other early modern accounts, such as by Thomas Hobbes), he still thinks we can cultivate certain habits that help us to bring our passions to some extent under our control. The idea that we ought not to be slaves, but masters of our passions is not unique to Descartes. As Pierre Hadot observes, it occurs in a wide range of philosophical traditions. With some exaggeration, he states, "One conception was common to all the philosophical schools: people are unhappy because they are the slave of their passions."[26]

Descartes's view of the passions is of continued relevance, because it can guide us to make the passions work for us. To put it in contemporary terms, we can see how we can modulate our emotions so that they help us learn about the world and be happier overall. *The Passions of the Soul* offers a framework to understand both how our emotions are an integral part of who we are, and the importance of cultivating and properly tempering them in order to lead meaningful lives. Throughout this book, I examine how we use cultural means to control our emotions, with a focus on awe and wonder. These cultural means I term *cognitive technologies*. They allow us to control ourselves and our environment, by changing how our mind engages with the world.

I take the Cartesian view of the passions in order to examine the role of awe and wonder in our lives. As we will see in more detail in the next chapter, Descartes considers awe and wonder (in French *admiration*) as a kind of *firstness*; specifically, *admiration* is "a sudden surprise of the soul which brings it to consider with attention the objects that seem to it unusual and extraordinary."[27] As I use the term here and elsewhere, my concept of firstness is inspired by and closely allied to Descartes's view of the function of wonder, but slightly expanded so as to allow for the idea that we wonder not only at what we apprehend for the first time, but also at what we apprehend when we *take the attitude* that it is happening for the first time. I will argue that cultivating this sense of firstness is essential for our acquisition of knowledge and for integrating this knowledge into meaningful, happy lives.

I part ways with Descartes in his view that we must, as soon as feasible, work to dampen our sense of wonder, rather than encourage it. Descartes believes that, though it might be useful to experience wonder for initial learning, we need subsequently to check this emotion. In contrast to Descartes, I think that it often pays off to cultivate one's sense of awe and wonder in appropriate circumstances, because it liberates us from existing thought patterns and ideas.

In chapters 2 and 3, I look at philosophical and psychological perspectives on awe and wonder. In chapter 2, I trace the development of the view that philosophy is born in wonder, devoting special attention to views on the passions in early modern philosophy. Chapter 3 places awe and wonder in an evolutionary context, examining how these emotions enrich our lives and help us to deal with the world.

Then, following the tradition of classic anthropology such as James Frazer's *Golden Bough*,[28] I focus on three human cognitive technologies that have been a source of puzzlement, indeed wonder: magic, religion, and science. At the heart of these lie our capacities to experience awe and wonder. Chapter 4 looks at magic, a domain of human culture that has traditionally received intense scrutiny and attention from anthropologists and psychologists, but that has lately been neglected. Magic centers on our ability (feigned or supposed) to work wonders. Practicing magic involves power and agency, as well as being passively receptive to the wondrous. Chapter 5 will consider religion as a cognitive technology that helps us to feel and rediscover awe and wonder. I use Maurice Merleau-Ponty's notion of skillful habits to show how religion can be conducive to these emotions. Chapter 6 looks at science, and the role awe plays in scientific practice. Guided by Jean-Paul Sartre's views on the emotions, I show that awe plays a crucial role in scientific creativity, and helps scientists to deal with the difficult business of paradigm change. Chapter 7 takes a closer look at Rachel Carson's views on wonder and its role in our moral dealings with the environment. Chapter 8 offers a reflection on why we should reclaim our sense of wonder.

Let me conclude this introduction with a brief note on the illustrations, one for each chapter in the book. My drawings hark back to a lost tradition: namely, that of philosophy done in the visual mode.[29] While we now tend to think of philosophy as a purely textual enterprise, early modern Europeans (roughly from the sixteenth to the eighteenth century) also philosophized in images. Their printed media included prints and frontispieces, such as Abraham Bosse's frontispiece for Thomas Hobbes's *Leviathan*, which depicts a giant figure with a scepter and crosier, composed of a mass of people, thereby visualizing the idea that the ruler can unite the interests of the people.[30] These were not merely decorative illustrations, but non-verbal commentaries on the philosophical ideas that helped the reader to think and to philosophize for themselves. My drawings in this book aim to do the same.

2

That Sudden Surprise of the Soul

HOW WONDER FUELS PHILOSOPHY

Philosophy Is Born in Wonder

Philosophers like to see themselves as dispassionate critical thinkers. Yet, they can and do get carried away, becoming intensely focused to the point of obsession on a philosophical idea or work. Take Nicolas Malebranche (1638–1715), who at the age of twenty-six happened to pick up René Descartes's posthumously published *Traité de l'homme* (*Treatise on Man*, an account of human physiology) in a Paris bookstall. Malebranche, who disliked the Aristotelian scholasticism he had been taught, found Descartes exhilarating. So head-over-heels was he that "the joy of learning such a great number of new discoveries caused palpitations of the heart that were so severe, that he had to stop reading regularly in order to breathe more easily."[1]

Philosophy is born in wonder, but philosophical theories can also themselves become a source of wonder. They do so by helping us see the world and what we believed we knew with different eyes. They give us a sense of firstness: namely, of seeing the familiar as wondrous or strange, as if we were encountering it for the first time. We get this sense of firstness in mundane situations, such as when a common word suddenly sounds bizarre, or a common sight suddenly appears alien. Some philosophers cultivate this firstness by encouraging us to consider the weirdness of situations we rarely pause to reflect on. Take David Hume's case of the billiard balls.[2] When you see a ball roll in a straight path toward another, you assume that it will strike that ball, and you infer that the first ball *causes* the other one to roll. But without having experienced similar collisions, you would not be able to predict this outcome. Hume's example suggests that causation is not something you transparently observe. Rather, all you see is a ball strike another ball, followed by movement of the struck ball. You infer, through experience, that one is the cause and the other the effect.

Other philosophers wonder at social conventions. Although our conventions and institutions seem like they're set in stone, in fact they are not, and we have the power to change them. We see this clearly in contemporary philosophy of sex, gender, and race, but also in older works. The ancient Chinese philosopher Zhuangzi (ca. 369–286 BCE) was sitting fishing when two state officials from the kingdom of Chu came to offer him a prestigious position as chief administrator. Without turning around, he said,

> I have heard that in Chu there is a sacred tortoise which died three thousand years ago. The ruler keeps it covered with a cloth in a hamper in his ancestral temple. What would you say that the tortoise would have preferred: to die and leave its shell to be venerated, or to live and keep on dragging its tail over the mud?[3]

The officials agreed it would rather be alive, so Zhuangzi concluded, "Go your ways. I will keep on dragging my tail over the mud." This is a startling response. For readers at the time, as now, turning down a cushy position like this, which comes with wealth and honor, would be virtually inconceivable. Zhuangzi evokes a sense of wonder and unfamiliarity by likening that position to being a desiccated tortoise carcass stored away in a box.

Although the ideas that interest philosophers don't often keep laypeople awake at night, everyone, regardless of their social class or education, has moments of quiet reflection and wonder: for example, we wonder about the amazing series of coincidences that led to us being born, whether there is life after death, or whether God exists. In that sense, we are all born philosophers. Ancient Greek philosophers claimed that philosophy begins in wonder. In the ancient Greek cultural context, philosophy had a much broader scope than it has in contemporary academia. It encompassed fields of study that now have their own dedicated scientific disciplines, such as biology, astronomy, and psychology. Philosophy sought answers to questions such as, Why do our molars seem shaped for grinding food and our incisors for cutting it? How did the universe originate? What's a comet? How does the eye work? What are the basic human emotions?

The intimate connection between wonder and philosophy is the focus of this chapter. In particular, I investigate the idea that wonder is a motivating passion that urges us to do philosophy, in both its ancient and its modern sense. As we'll see, especially since the early modern period (since the late sixteenth century), philosophers have employed an increasingly rich and nuanced vocabulary to think about wonder, distinguishing different kinds of wonder, and differentiating wonder from awe. In earlier sources, awe and wonder were denoted by the same words, including *thaumazein* in Greek and *admiratio* in Latin. The historical context is important to understand their continued role in philosophy. With this in mind, I present a bird's eye view of the precursors to our notions of awe and wonder in Western philosophy through works by Plato, Aristotle, Descartes, and Adam Smith.

Thaumazein and *admiratio* in Ancient Greek and Medieval Philosophy

Plato and Aristotle made a connection between wonder and philosophy. The words that translate as wonder or awe are *thauma* and related concepts such as *thaumazôn*. As philologist Glen Most observes, in epic ancient Greek literature *thauma* denotes joyous, overwhelmed surprise.[4] It is closely related to perception. Its etymology likely traces back to the verb *theaomai*, "to gaze upon" or "contemplate," originally by an official spectator at religious ceremonies. In epic Greek poetry, "wonder" denotes astonished surprise at an object or a person (often a god), not at an event. Later, the term was generalized to observation of events and contemplation of problems and abstract questions. The valence of *thauma* is positive: it is the surprise, joy, and admiration we may feel when we are confronted with a specific object or person.

We see a shift in the concept of wonder in Plato's *Theaetetus* (written around 369 BCE), a dialogue between the philosopher Socrates, the brilliant young mathematician Theaetetus, and his tutor Theodorus. Their conversation focuses on the question, "What is knowledge?" Socrates avows that he doesn't know what knowledge is. Perhaps Theaetetus can shed light on the matter? Socrates proposes he will be a midwife, helping Theaetetus give birth to wisdom. Theaetetus ventures some definitions of knowledge, three of which are discussed in detail: knowledge is perception, true judgment, and true judgment with an account. But, as he is apt to do, Socrates presents counterexamples and difficulties for each of these definitions, and the dialogue ends without a satisfactory definition of knowledge.

Early in the dialogue, Theaetetus expresses his feelings of perplexity and physical dizziness as he navigates the barrage of questions and objections Socrates launches:

> THEAETETUS: Yes, Socrates, and I perpetually wonder—by the gods I do!—how to make sense of it all; sometimes just looking at it makes me literally quite dizzy.
>
> SOCRATES: My friend, it appears Theodorus' guess about your nature wasn't far wrong. This wondering of yours is very much the mark of a philosopher—philosophy starts nowhere else but with wondering [*to thaumazein*], and the man who made Iris the offspring of Thaumas wasn't far off with his genealogy.[5]

Here, Plato confirms the epistemic character of wonder. The genealogy Plato refers to is a pseudo-etymology between *Thaumas* and *thauma* in Hesiod's writings. The connection with Iris is somewhat more puzzling, but Most speculates that Iris is the messenger who brings divine announcements to humans.[6] Iris is also the goddess and personification of the rainbow, a meteorological phenomenon that is a frequent source of wonder. As the mediator between gods and humans, she embodies the activity of philosophy itself, for philosophy is our insatiable human desire for a divine wisdom that we can never fully attain but always strive for. It is fitting that this overall dialogue ends in *aporia*, a state of puzzlement: despite all of Theaetetus's proposals, we still don't know what knowledge is.

Aristotle (384–322 BCE), Plato's student, also saw wonder as central to philosophy, but with an interesting twist. Born in Stagira, northern Greece, to a well-off family, Aristotle believed that the contemplative life was the privilege of a very small, select elite: namely, wealthy, free-born men. Throughout his writings, his contempt for people of lower social class, for slaves, and for women is clear. Yet, in spite of this elitism, Aristotle believed that the drive to philosophize was given to *all* people, not only to philosophers. In the *Metaphysics*, he argues that all philosophy comes from a universal desire to know:

> It is because of wondering at things [*to thaumazein*] that humans, both now and at first, began to do philosophy. At the start, they wondered [*thaumasantes*] at those of the puzzles that were close to hand, then, advancing little by little, they puzzled over greater issues, for example, about the attributes of the moon and about issues concerning the sun and stars, and how the universe comes to be. Someone who puzzles or wonders [*thaumazôn*], however, thinks himself ignorant (it

> is because of this, indeed, that the philosopher is in a way a mythlover, since myth is composed of wonders). So if indeed it was because of [a desire] to avoid ignorance that they engaged in philosophy, it is evident that it was because of [a desire] to know that they pursued scientific knowledge, and not for the sake of some sort of utility.[7]

Aristotle connects wonder to a desire to know and ultimately to wisdom (*sophia*), one of the core topics of the *Metaphysics*. He is concerned with "first philosophy," or the most foundational philosophy. We begin by wondering at everyday phenomena and puzzles, such as, "Why did the vase break when I dropped it?" Starting from such simple questions, we move on to ever more perplexing mysteries, including the origin of the universe, a puzzle that has gripped philosophers and scientists to this day.

In Aristotle's view, wonder lies at the basis not only of science and philosophy, but also of myth. In the ancient Greek context, this connects wonder to poetry, and what we would now call religion (both of these are encapsulated in the concept of myth). The myth-lover is also a lover of wisdom; Aristotle thus connects religion, science, art, and philosophy to our desire to know, which is born out of wonder. While the reasons for which we do all these things cannot be reduced to a single emotion, Aristotle suggests that wonder provides an important impulse. A wonderer realizes they are ignorant, and from this ignorance is born the desire to know. This desire to know gives rise to philosophical ideas, scientific concepts, theological constructs, and story-telling.

Like the ancient Greeks, medieval scholars also had an interest in wonder. Medievalist Caroline Walker Bynum argues that medieval scholars were interested in *admiratio* (a term that encompasses both awe and wonder).[8] *Admiratio* is rooted in Aristotle's idea of wonder as the source of our desire to know. It is subjective and perspectival: late classical thinkers such as Augustine (354–430) and medieval writers such as Thomas Aquinas (1225–1274) realized that a lot of our wonder is born from ignorance about how the world works. The ancient Greek and medieval concept of *thaumazein/admiratio* provides a unifying framework for science, religion, and art. These are responses to our sense of joyful contemplation of whatever we find unusual, surprising, and astounding. This idea is echoed in the analysis of wonder by Jesse Prinz. Prinz places wonder at the center of human pursuits and argues that "science, religion and art are unified in wonder. Each engages our senses, elicits curiosity and instils reverence. Without wonder, it is hard to believe that we would engage in these distinctively human pursuits."[9]

Early modern philosophers developed the idea of passions as motivators and devoted some attention to awe and wonder. For early scientists, awe and wonder are closely connected. They helped them to explore the wider vistas they were confronted with: distant countries, faraway solar systems, and the alien world under the microscope.

Microscopic and Macroscopic Marvels

In 1665, the Royal Society of London published a stunning book, *Micrographia*. The development of novel instruments such as telescopes and microscopes led to a radical rethinking of what the world is like. *Micrographia* features over thirty detailed engravings plus descriptions of a wide range of objects under the microscope, including mites, lice, fleas, mold, and urine crystals, thus giving the wealthy broader public a first glimpse into the world of tiny things.

The author, Robert Hooke (1635–1703), was curator of experiments of the Royal Society. Hooke was a talented draughtsman (apprenticed to the painter Peter Lely). He was an early scientist as well as an architect. He designed and constructed both telescopes and microscopes. In its preface, the *Micrographia* contains a set of instructions for how to build your own microscope, including which lenses to use.[10]

The intricacy of Hooke's pictures is dazzling. He drew, among other things, a large, fold-out image of a flea, praising its "strength and beauty." While the microscope could not reveal more about the flea's strength than people already knew with unaided perception (fleas are fearsome jumpers), its beauty was only now revealed: "the Microscope manifests it to be all over adorn'd with a curiously polish'd suit of sable armour, neatly jointed, and beset with multitudes of sharp pinns, shap'd almost like Porcupine's Quills, or bright conical Steel-bodkins."[11]

By contrast, human-made objects look surprisingly imperfect under the uncompromising focus of the microscope. The point of a needle is blunt, a razor blade so rough that it "would scarcely have serv'd to cleave wood, much less to have cut off the hair of beards."[12] *Micrographia* was among the first scientific bestsellers. Its detailed engravings opened an amazing world to its audience. In the style of cosmographias, books that chart the world in the midst of colonial expansion and discovery by European explorers, *Micrographia* took the microscope and mapped out the minuscule in our everyday world. It will "make us, with the great Conqueror [Alexander], to be affected that we have not yet overcome one World when there are so many others to be discovered, every considerable improvement of Telescopes or Microscopes producing new Worlds and Terra-Incognita's to our view."[13]

Micrographia also opened to its audience an emotional world: one of awe and wonder including that unmistakable sense of horror that often accompanies the sublime. Mites look like terrifying mastodons, mold swells like lush mushrooms. We still feel this way when first looking through a (decent) microscope, if we're lucky enough to have a well-stocked science lab at school. In his preface, Hooke expressed optimism that humans can overcome their cognitive limitations through instruments such as telescopes and microscopes. As was common at the time, he believed that our senses and reason had been negatively affected by the Fall from the Garden of Eden, as described in Genesis 3. But thanks to our scientific instruments, we could restore what had been lost:

> And as at first, mankind fell by tasting of the forbidden Tree of Knowledge, so we, their Posterity, may be in part restor'd by the same way, not only by beholding and contemplating, but by tasting too those fruits of Natural knowledge, that were never yet forbidden.[14]

What Hooke didn't bargain for is that lenses don't just improve our vision; they can lead us to rethink who we are, and open worlds we previously weren't aware of.

During the same era, introduction of telescopes had a similar effect—it expanded people's vision to get a clearer picture of the solar system and beyond to many more worlds, potentially inhabited by alien life.

The French science popularizer and early Enlightenment thinker Bernard le Bovier de Fontenelle (1657–1757) explored the implications of the telescope in his *Conversations on the Plurality of Worlds* (*Entretiens sur la pluralité des mondes*, 1686).[15] The book is styled as a novel.[16]

Conversations takes place over five evenings, and records tête-à-têtes between an unnamed philosopher (who is also the narrator) and an uneducated, but intelligent, unnamed Marquise as they stroll through her gardens in the moonlight. The starting point of these conversations is an idle speculation by the philosopher that "every star could be a world. I wouldn't swear that it's true, but I think so, because it pleases me to think so."[17] In the seventeenth century in this context, "world" usually meant "solar system," as early scientists and philosophers were taking in the full implications of the Copernican revolution.

Telescopes helped to answer questions, but also raised a host of new ones. While they showed Jupiter had moons, they weren't powerful enough to establish intelligent alien life in our solar system or beyond, nor the existence of exoplanets. The early moderns looked at the moon with yearning—so close, yet so unreachable! Thus, as the philosopher remarks, "All philosophy [. . .] is based on two things only: curiosity and poor eyesight; if you had better eyesight you could see perfectly well whether or not these stars are solar systems, and if you were less curious you wouldn't care about knowing."[18] Early modern authors invented fantastical tales of what life on the moon would be like. The astronomer Johannes Kepler wrote a short novel, *Somnium* (*Dream*), published posthumously in 1634, which features the Icelandic witch Fiolxhilde and her son Duracotus who visit the moon and its strange realms by communing with daemons. Soon thereafter followed the publications of Francis Godwin's *Man in the Moon* (1638) and Cyrano de Bergerac's *The Other World: Comical History of the States and Empires of the Moon* (*L'Autre Monde, ou Les États et Empires de la lune*) (1657). Cyrano de Bergerac paid some attention to the practicalities of reaching the moon. The narrator (also named Cyrano) makes several attempts to reach the moon, including one by means of bottles of dew strapped to his body, and eventually succeeds with a kind of rocket. So by the time Fontenelle's *Conversations* was published, science fiction stories featuring the moon were an established genre in France and elsewhere in Europe.

Fontenelle's characters spend their second evening discussing the possibility of life on the moon. However, they don't stop there. The third and fourth evenings' discussions feature life on the other planets of the solar system. Eventually, during the fifth evening, the characters discuss the possibility of life in other solar systems. This widening of the universe gives rise to a sense of mental vertigo. The Marquise objects,

> here is a universe so large that I'm lost, I no longer know where I am, I'm nothing [. . .]. Each star will be the center of a vortex, perhaps as large as ours?[19] All this immense space which holds our Sun and our planets will be merely a small piece of the universe? As many spaces as there are fixed stars? This confounds me—troubles me—terrifies me.[20]

The philosopher replies,

> This puts me at my ease. When the sky was only this blue vault, with the stars nailed to it, the universe seemed small and narrow to me; I felt oppressed by it. Now that they've given infinitely greater breadth and depth to this vault by dividing it into thousands and thousands of vortices, it seems to me that I breathe more freely, that I'm in a larger air.[21]

This reveals a tension between what psychologists now call negative and positive awe; I will discuss this in the next chapter. The realization that the universe is huge can lead to a sense of self-annihilation and horror, but it can also give a sense of freedom and a cosmopolitan optimism, a sense that we are all interconnected and part of a wondrous universe.

The wonder evoked by this expanding universe at the microscopic and macroscopic level thus leads to self-contemplation. As we will see in more detail in the next chapter, one of the central features of awe and wonder is the cognitive need for accommodation, which is the realization that our familiar frameworks and heuristics do not work anymore. In the absence of our usual ways of thinking, we need to rethink our place in the world. In a passage in the *Pensées* (1670) that discusses these two newly found levels of the universe, scientist, mathematician, and philosopher Blaise Pascal (1623–1662) reflects on the wonders that telescopes and microscopes reveal, both the vast and the tiny.[22] At first, we're invited to contemplate the whole of nature, and the limits of what telescopes can show us:

> Let the earth seem to him [humanity] like a point in comparison with the vast orbit described by that star. And let him be amazed that this vast orbit is itself but a very small point in comparison with the one described by the stars rolling around the firmament [. . .]. This whole visible world is only an imperceptible trace in the amplitude of nature.[23]

Pascal then invites the reader to consider a mite with its tiny body that shows "incomparably more minute parts, legs with joints, veins in its legs, blood in its veins, humors in this blood, drops in the humors, vapors in these drops."[24] You can just go on until your thought is exhausted and you can't imagine anything of an even smaller scale. This might lead you to think the scaling down ends there, but you would be wrong:

> I want to make him [humanity] see a new abyss in there. I want to depict for him not just the visible universe, but the immensity of nature we can conceive inside the boundaries

> of this compact atom. Let him see there an infinity of universes, each with its firmament, its planets, its earth, in the same proportion as in the visible world; and on this earth animals, and finally mites, where he will find again what he saw before, and find still in the others the same thing without end and without cessation. Let him lose himself in wonders as astonishing in their minuteness as the others are in their extent! [i.e., the universe in its grandeur] For who will not marvel that our body, imperceptible a little while ago in the universe, itself imperceptible inside the totality, should now be a colossus, a world, or rather a whole, with respect to the nothingness beyond our reach?[25]

More recent exercises along these lines are the two documentaries entitled *Powers of Ten* made by Charles and Ray Eames (from 1968 and 1977; many versions exist online), where you can see a couple having a picnic zoomed in (on the hand of the man, down to molecules and atoms) and zoomed out (to the earth, solar system, Milky Way, and galaxy clusters). We no longer tend to think of the world of tiny things as harboring infinite universes within universes like a series of Russian dolls. Nevertheless, the quantum world is a very strange world indeed.[26]

Pascal uses the sense of vertigo caused by telescopes and microscopes as a rhetorical device.[27] Thinking of the vast and the minute inevitably leads to self-contemplation: "Where do I fit in nature?" The widening scope of the telescopic and microscopic squeezes humanity between two abysses:

> Whoever considers himself in this way will be afraid of himself, and, seeing himself supported by the size nature has given him between these two abysses of the infinite and nothingness, he will tremble at these marvels. I believe that, as his curiosity changes into admiration [Fr. *admiration*, i.e.,

> wonder], he will be more disposed to contemplate them in silence than to examine them with presumption. For, in the end, what is man in nature? A nothing compared to the infinite, an everything compared to the nothing, a midpoint between nothing and everything, infinitely removed from understanding the extremes [. . .]. *[What then will he be able to conceive? He is]* equally incapable of seeing the nothingness from which he derives and the infinite in which he is engulfed.[28]

In this passage, Pascal distinguishes between curiosity and wonder ("curiosité se changeant en admiration") as two distinct intellectual passions: curiosity is a fickle passion of fleeting interest, wonder a more enduring disposition. We see a similar contrast between curiosity (uniformly negative) and wonder (appropriate under some conditions) in Descartes as well.[29]

Hooke, Fontenelle, and Pascal show the importance of wonder as a starting point for philosophical contemplation for early modern philosophers. Science doesn't diminish the sense of wonder, but fans its flames, because it inevitably leads us to contemplate ourselves and our place in the world. Early modern authors also saw wonder as a passion that can be stirred and evoked in a wide range of settings. We see it in popularizing science, as written by Hooke and Fontenelle, but also in theater and opera, politics, magic, and early science. Early modern interest in the passions and mood-managing techniques based on them such as rhetoric and musical harmony came from the following observation: in any given situation people don't react in objective terms, but based on how they feel.[30] Feelings sometimes trump facts, and while feelings are real, they are not always apt. This forms the basis for many early modern theater plot devices, wherein passions and misunderstandings lead the characters to commit grave mistakes, such as Othello's murder of his wife Desdemona and Romeo and Juliet's double suicide. It is unsurprising then, that we see major philosophical theorizing on this, by authors such as Hobbes, Descartes, Spinoza, and many others.

Descartes: Wonder as That Sudden Surprise of the Soul

In *The Passions of the Soul* (*Les Passions de l'âme*, 1649), philosopher, mathematician, and early scientist René Descartes (1596–1650) argued for the centrality of wonder in the pursuit of knowledge. This is Descartes's final work, published while he worked as a tutor for Queen Christina in Sweden. It is dedicated to his philosophical friend and long-term correspondent Princess Elisabeth of Bohemia. His theory of the passions is his answer to Elisabeth's challenge: "How do soul and body interact with each other?" Descartes held that the soul is immaterial and rational, and that the body is material and purely mechanical, two entirely different substances that make up a person. If that is true, Elisabeth objected, it seems hard to conceive how our mental states would be affected by the material world. According to Descartes, the passions are one way in which the material body affects the immaterial soul. They are physical phenomena in our bodies that inform the soul of the potential utility or harm of an object or event. They focus our attention upon relevant features of our environment. This gives them a crucial role both in our cognition and in the way we lead our lives.

A "passion of the soul" is a mental state that arises as a direct result of brain activity. (Descartes erroneously believed that the point of interaction of body and soul where passions move the soul is the pineal gland, an endocrine gland in the brain.

We now know that it is mainly involved in regulating our circadian rhythms by producing melatonin when it is dark.) The passions are material, though their job is to inform the immaterial soul, which can make rational decisions based on their input. However, they can also cause us to take inappropriate action: for instance, when we do something in a fit of anger that we later regret. The material substrate of the passions consists of what Descartes terms "animal spirits," which are roughly analogous to our nervous system; they are also involved in muscle movement and run throughout the body. Physiology, specifically in early modern Europe was in an early stage of development, and the nervous system wasn't well understood. Descartes posited six basic passions: wonder (in early modern French *admiration*, derived from the Latin *admiratio*), love, hatred, desire, joy, and sadness. All other passions you experience are either composites of these, or variations on them.[31]

Wonder is the first passion, because we experience it when we first encounter an object or event and before we make a judgment about whether it is good or bad for us: "Since all this [wonder] may happen before we know whether or not the object is beneficial to us, I regard wonder as the first of all the passions."[32] As Perry Zurn writes, "Cartesian wonder is a passion before judgment, which nevertheless *demands* judgment."[33] Judgment will come once our sense of wonder dissipates, and the other passions take over. Descartes defines wonder as follows:

> Wonder is a sudden surprise of the soul which brings it to consider with attention the objects that seem to it unusual and extraordinary.[34]

He discerns two causes for wonder: an impression in the brain of an unusual object or event that we deem worthy of consideration, and "a movement of the spirits through which we locate the impression and preserve it in the brain."[35] Descartes explicitly locates wonder only in the brain, "in which are located the organs of the senses used in gaining this knowledge [of the object or event we wonder at]."[36] This is in contrast with the other passions, whereby the animal spirits also cause other physiological changes in heart rate and blood pressure. Experiencing wonder does not change heart rate and blood pressure, making it the least carnal and literally the most cerebral of passions, though it can still be violent due to its element of surprise. Descartes argues that unlike other passions, wonder "has as its object not good or evil, but only knowledge of the thing that we wonder at."[37] To put it differently, wonder does not lead us to appraise negatively or positively the object or event we wonder at, unlike the other passions. For example, we tend to see things that makes us happy in a positive light, and things that make us sad in a negative light. When we wonder at something, we have not yet examined how it can be used (or misused). We simply meet it on its own terms. Wonder is thus a provisional passion.

What is the use of wonder? For Descartes, the passions inform the rational soul. The passions are a physiological response to our sensory impressions (impressions on the brain), accord a valence (positive, negative, or surprising) to situations we encounter, and then motivate us to act on the basis of these inputs.[38] Wonder doesn't make positive or negative evaluations; rather, it focuses our attention on things that we don't know yet:

> [wonder] is useful in that it makes us learn and retain in our memory things of which we were previously ignorant. For we wonder only at what appears to us unusual and extraordinary; and something can appear so only because we have been ignorant of it, or perhaps because it differs from things we have known.[39]

Without passions to strengthen our memory, we would quickly forget the new information. Hence, "we see that people who are not naturally inclined to wonder are usually very ignorant."[40]

We can contrast this view with that of another early modern philosopher. In his *Short Treatise on God, Man, and His Well-Being* (ca. 1661), Benedictus (Baruch) de Spinoza (1632–1677) also treats wonder as the first passion. In Spinoza's early account, wonder (*verwondering*) arises when reality does not accord with our preconceptions. For example, someone who has always seen Dutch sheep which have short tails is astonished at the sight of a Moroccan sheep, which has a long tail. They start out with the wrong idea that all sheep have short tails, but as Spinoza remarks, "there is no wonder in him who draws true conclusions"; namely, sheep can have either short or long tails.[41] For Descartes, by contrast, wonder does not arise so much from erroneous preconceptions, as from a lack of earlier experience. In the posthumously published *Ethics* (part 3) Spinoza no longer numbers wonder as one of the primary affects, having reduced these to just three: joy, sadness, and desire.[42]

Although Descartes recognizes that passions help us to regulate our behavior in various ways—for example, by motivating us to learn about our environment—he cautions against letting the passions rule our decisions. Shoshana Brassfield points to numerous passages in *Passions* in which Descartes argues that we should train our passions, much like a hunting dog can be trained to not be startled by a gun shot.[43] If we can train an animal (which Descartes believed to be devoid of reason), then certainly we can train ourselves: "There is no soul so weak that it cannot, if well-directed, acquire an absolute power over its passions."[44] In the case of wonder, "although it is good to be born with some inclination to wonder, since it makes us disposed to acquire scientific knowledge, yet after acquiring such knowledge, we must attempt to free ourselves from this inclination as much as possible."[45] Descartes thinks that undifferentiated wonder is unhelpful as it does not allow us to distinguish between those objects that merit attention and mere curiosities of no importance. The cleverest people are not those who wonder most or least, but who wonder to an appropriate extent, and who reflect upon the things they have wondered at.

Thus, wonder is a good starting point of inquiry and for retention of new information in our memory, but once we have learned more about what we first wondered at, it is altogether better that we should not keep on wondering. As we saw, for Aristotle knowledge is also the terminal point of wonder. In this respect, Descartes's account of wonder sharply differs from that of more recent theorists of wonder such as Abraham Heschel, Rachel Carson, or Michelle Shiota, who think we should maintain a continued sense of awe and wonder, including at the *end* of our inquiry. In early modernity, we can also find authors who think that scientific inquiry not only begins, but also ends in wonder, in particular Adam Smith (see next section).

Zurn shows how Descartes's conception of wonder is intimately tied to his approach to philosophy, pedagogy, and science.[46] Educators at the time assumed that learning a lot of facts through reading books would suffice for a student's expertise. Want to be a mathematician? Just read a lot of mathematics books and learn the contents by heart! Descartes worried that rote learning can injure education.

Instead, pedagogy should emulate divine instruction, which is the embodied process of learning by interacting with nature. To this end, Descartes wants to capture the strangeness and wondrousness of nature in his writings, for example in *The World* (*Le Monde*):

> I do not promise to set out exact demonstrations of everything I shall say. It will be enough if I open the way which will enable you to discover them yourselves, when you take the trouble to look for them. Most minds lose interest when things are made too easy for them. And to present a picture which pleases you, I need to use shadow as well as bright colors. So I shall be content to continue with the description I have begun, as if my intention was simply to tell you a fable.[47]

Reading philosophy is, in Descartes's view, akin to being taken on an adventure:

> When we read of strange adventures in a book, or see them acted out on the stage, this sometimes arouses sadness in us, sometimes joy, or love, or hatred, and generally any of the passions [. . .]. But we have pleasure in feeling them aroused in us, and this pleasure is an intellectual joy.[48]

Wonder may give us an impulse to knowledge, but to put in the hard work of learning, we also need other motivators, such as a love for knowledge, and willpower. At the end of scientific inquiry, we should cease to wonder. As Brown puts it, for Descartes, "the works of God leave us in awe but not wonderstruck."[49]

Adam Smith on Wonder: "that uncertainty and anxious curiosity"

The History of Astronomy (1795) is a posthumously published essay by the Scottish economic theorist and philosopher Adam Smith (1723–1790). Although Smith is now best known for the ideas about the economy, free markets, and self-interest he set out in his *Wealth of Nations* (1776), he is also the author of several works on human sentiments and their role in our moral and epistemic lives. In *The Theory of Moral Sentiments*, first published in 1759, he adopts a Humean framework whereby sentiments are held to be motivators for action. Even if we can use reason to determine the best course of action, it's our sentiments (Smith's term for emotions) that lead us to perform (or not perform) an action.

Smith argued against authors such as Bernard Mandeville (1670–1733) and Thomas Hobbes (1588–1679) who thought that people are fundamentally self-interested, and that our morality, and more generally culture, can be explained as a result of self-interested actions. Smith objected by putting sympathy at the heart of his account. Sympathy (what we'd now call empathy) is fellow-feeling with others. It is the glue that holds social groups together. Society is not just a safety net that we use to escape the state of nature, but something we are drawn into because we need and desire human company. This is in stark contrast with Mandeville, who believed that our culture (technology, art, etc.) is ultimately driven by purely selfish motives. It also contradicts Hobbes, who believed that morality is the same as prudence, whereby your main motivation for acting morally is to not get yourself in a pickle.

The History of Astronomy continues Smith's project of trying to understand how human cultures are fundamentally motivated by sentiments. An unsuspecting reader might think the book would do as the title suggests—namely, give a historical account of astronomy, a science with an especially significant history in the period leading up to the time when Smith was writing. However, its first three sections (out of a total of four) are about our emotional motivations to practice astronomy, and how scientific explanations are structured. Smith regards astronomy as a practice that responds to our epistemic sentiments. Because we stare at the night sky, and we wonder at why the heavenly bodies move the way they do, we engage in astronomical theorizing. We wonder at rare events such as eclipses and appearances of comets, and struggle to give these anomalous events a place in our general picture of the universe.

This sense of wonder is, for Smith, a *negative* emotion: it feels unpleasant to wonder. This is in contrast to Descartes, who believes wonder is a neutral emotion, leading neither to positive nor negative appraisals. Smith thinks that whenever we are confronted with something wondrous, we experience a strong physiological reaction:

> [t]he sentiment properly called *Wonder* [. . . :] that staring, and some times that rolling of the eyes, that suspension of the breath, and that swelling of the heart, which we may all observe, both in ourselves and others, when wondering at some new object, and which are the natural symptoms of uncertain and undetermined thought.[50]

We come up with scientific explanations that help us make sense of anomalous astronomical observations, and thus help assuage our sense of wonder. Take Kirch's Comet, which passed in close proximity to Earth on November 30, 1680. It was so bright it could be seen by day, and it had a spectacularly long tail. It inspired numerous paintings, even musical compositions, and gave rise to astronomical speculations.[51] Spectacular astronomical sightings like these, as well as other natural phenomena, evoke a sense of wonder. Smith provides a fine-grained taxonomy of intellectual sentiments to distinguish wonder from surprise and admiration:

> Wonder, Surprise, and Admiration, are words which, though often confounded, denote, in our language, sentiments that

> are indeed allied, but that are in some respects different also, and distinct from one another. What is new and singular, excites that sentiment which, in strict propriety, is called Wonder; what is unexpected, Surprise; and what is great or beautiful, Admiration.[52]

Smith goes on,

> We wonder at all extraordinary and uncommon objects, at all the rarer phænomena of nature, at meteors, comets, eclipses, at singular plants and animals, and at every thing, in short, with which we have before been either little or not at all acquainted; and we will still wonder, though forewarned of what we are to see.[53]

In Smith's taxonomy of intellectual sentiments, surprise is the primary emotion. It is our immediate reaction to something unexpected; it is the most sudden and violent. For example, when you meet a friend you have not seen in a long time, you may be surprised, but you do not wonder because (to put it in contemporary terms) there is nothing in your expectations that makes this exceptional. When what we encounter remains inexplicable, we feel wonder. Suppose you have emigrated to another country, and all of a sudden, a friend from school stands on your porch. You are both surprised and you wonder, because there is nothing in your expectations to see an old friend from school in a foreign land in front of your door. Admiration is similar, but also has a clear aesthetic component in that it is reserved for something beautiful and great. In this way, Smith departs from the ancient Greek *thauma* and Descartes's *admiration*. Early modern English seems to allow for a subtler distinction, disentangling wonder from both admiration and surprise.

But Smith does not only follow English linguistic conventions, as he further distinguishes two kinds of wonder. One kind occurs when we are confronted with something unexpected that defies categorization. A second kind of wonder "arises from an unusual succession of things. The stop which is thereby given to the career of the imagination, the difficulty which it finds in passing along such disjointed objects, and the feeling of something like a gap or interval betwixt them, constitute the whole essence of this emotion."[54] Here, it is not so much the objects themselves that defy our categorization as the relationships between them.

Eric Schliesser interprets Smith's account of wonder in an almost pragmatist sense: wonder is an unpleasant emotion that drives us to seek knowledge, because the incongruities that give rise to our sense of wonder stand in the way of mental tranquility: "this natural history reveals [. . .] that while the fundamental aim of inquiry may be mental repose or tranquility, Smith conceives of the intellectual sentiments as being action-oriented."[55] This is similar to American pragmatists, such as C. S. Peirce, who see belief as the default state we strive to maintain, and doubt as an unpleasant upset.[56] In Peirce's view, much like Smith's, the aim of inquiry is to get back to that state of belief, which is calm and pleasant.

Smith examines how this sense of wonder at meteorological and astronomical phenomena constitutes the basis of philosophy and religion. Like Hume, he attributes the origin of polytheism to observations of irregularities in nature, such as droughts, tempests, or headwaters of rivers.[57] Because people had a sensation of wonder at unusual events in nature, they invented gods who were behind these events. Polytheistic religions are the earliest attempts to make rational sense of the world in response to our sense of wonder. Smith goes on to argue that philosophy begins the moment people have some leisure and are no longer occupied with the mere task of survival. He almost reiterates the excerpt of Aristotle's *Metaphysics* we saw earlier in this chapter, concluding,

> Wonder, therefore, and not any expectation of advantage from its discoveries, is the first principle which prompts mankind to the study of Philosophy, of that science which pretends to lay open the concealed connections that unite the various appearances of nature; and they pursue this study for its own sake, as an original pleasure or good in itself, without regarding its tendency to procure them the means of many other pleasures.[58]

Like philosophy, the sciences are born from a sense of wonder. Smith considers a naturalist who examines with curious attention "a singular plant, or a singular fossil that is presented to him."[59] When Smith wrote in the late eighteenth century, the increasing number and diversity of fossils had begun to challenge natural classification schemes that saw biological organisms as fixed and unchanging. Moreover, Smith was a member of the same dining club as James Hutton (1726–1797), one of the founders of modern geology, who used fossil evidence to argue that the world was a great deal older than six thousand years. The naturalist will do his best to "get rid of that Wonder, that uncertainty and anxious curiosity excited by its singular appearance, and by its dissimilitude with all the objects he had hitherto observed."[60] If, to the best of his efforts, he is unable to place the fossil or new specimen into his classification scheme, his sense of wonder remains.

Likewise, astronomy arises from the sense of wonder at the night sky. Particularly, the sense of the unexpected, the inability to categorize, is evoked in us by astronomical phenomena such as comets and eclipses, which interrupt the regularity of moving bodies in the sky. In his historical account of astronomy, Smith puzzlingly denies the practical reasons for astronomy (such as using the stars for sea navigation), which must have been known to him. Instead, he focuses on how astronomical systems, such as Ptolemy's spheres, were invented to help cease our sense of wonder at the night sky. Those astronomical systems, in turn, became a source of wonder and admiration: "if it gained the belief of mankind by its plausibility, it attracted their wonder and admiration; sentiments that still more confirmed their belief, by the novelty and beauty of that view of nature which it presented to the imagination."[61]

The History of Astronomy is full of inaccuracies about the actual history of astronomy, but it is of continued interest because of the central importance of emotions as motivators. Smith recognized that scientists are not purely driven by evidential reasons in their adoption of new theories and paradigms.[62] The aim of philosophers and early scientists is to decrease our sense of wonder:

> Philosophy is the science of the connecting principles of nature [. . .] by representing the invisible chains which bind together all these disjointed objects, endeavours to introduce order into this chaos of jarring and discordant appearances, to allay this tumult of the imagination and to restore it, when it surveys the great revolutions of the universe, to that tone of tranquility and composure, which is both most agreeable in itself and most suitable to its nature.[63]

In Smith's view, philosophy and science do not end the state of wonder. Rather, as they present us with order and help us to make sense of the world, they offer new possibilities to see anomalies. A detailed new classification scheme for organisms or a new astronomical system allows for wonder because wonder does not happen when we are presented with pure chaos, but rather, with violations of our expectations.[64] Imagine the naturalist, who gazes upon a puzzling fossil such as a trilobite or ammonite. The fossil doesn't clearly fit the elaborate Linnean classification scheme and thus elicits wonder. This wonder could be caused because the fossil has anatomical features that don't fit within natural history, or because the features do not appear in an arrangement the naturalist expects. Our orderly classification scheme breaks down when we are presented with anomalies. This is what causes wonder, an epistemic irritation we want to get rid of. Thus, science also creates wonder: if we had not tried to classify organisms in a neat classificatory system, we would never have noticed the anomalies of the fossil specimen in front of us. To notice irregularity, one needs order and regularity in the first place. In this respect, Smith anticipates Thomas Kuhn's account of scientific revolutions.[65] Our sense of wonder ultimately forces us to alter our scientific theories (I will go more into this in chapter 6).

In contrast to Descartes, Smith predicts that there will never be a state when we will cease wondering. There will always be new questions that will awaken the sense of wonder within us, and that we will try to satisfy. Philosophy both begins and ends in wonder. It begins our philosophical speculations, and still motivates our most detailed scientific endeavors, and will keep on popping up whenever we are confronted with something that violates our expectations. Smith evokes the image of nature as an opera-house, a metaphor that also occurs in Fontenelle's *Conversations*: "Who wonders at the machinery of the opera-house who has once been admitted behind the scenes? In the wonders of nature, however, it rarely happens that we can discover so clearly this connecting chain."[66]

3

Mysteries of the Mind

THE PSYCHOLOGY OF AWE AND WONDER

The Psychological Study of Emotions

As we've seen in the previous chapter, ancient Greek, medieval, and early modern philosophers believed that awe and wonder help us to gain knowledge. These emotions alert us to what we don't know, and motivate us to learn more. In this chapter,

I consider evolutionary and psychological theories on emotions. Like other emotions, awe and wonder help us to be more effective in our dealings with our environment. They inform our thinking and shape our actions. Awe and wonder do this by challenging what we think we know. They not only motivate us to learn more about the world, but also encourage self-reflection and how we should think of ourselves as inhabiting a vast, strange, and, indeed, wondrous universe.

I begin by outlining how emotions help biological organisms to respond effectively to the world they inhabit. I then present an influential evolutionary picture of emotions, which holds that humans (like other animals) only have a small repertoire of basic emotions that have evolved in response to adaptive problems. Next, I look at the limitations of this picture: we have complex emotions that are not direct, evolved responses to adaptive problems. How should we think of their function? Through our cultural means such as music, literature, social conventions, and architecture, humans have developed a more extensive emotional repertoire that goes significantly beyond, though it builds on, their basic emotions. I hypothesize that awe and wonder are not basic emotions, though they are biologically significant. They help us to deal with situations that challenge what we think we know.

Contemporary psychology builds on a rich philosophical tradition of theorizing on emotions, some of which we saw in the previous chapter. Most psychologists hold that emotions are mental states that inform us about the world.[1] Beyond this, there are two main strands of thinking. On the one hand, *cognitivists* (such as Descartes) think that emotions are constitutive of evaluative judgments. When we're angry, we perceive something in our environment that incites us to feel anger at it. On the other hand, *non-cognitivists*, such as William James think that emotions amount to being aware of bodily states, such as when one shakes with grief or anger—the emotion is our physical, bodily awareness of that shaking and not so much an intellectual appraisal of something that's grief- or anger-inducing.[2] I don't aim to resolve this debate, and just note that many contemporary philosophers recognize that both aspects are important: emotions are both evaluative and embodied.[3]

Emotions are intentional, that is, they are directed at an object or situation. Introspect on what happens when you watch a magician who makes an elephant disappear. Your attention is drawn to its disappearance: you feel a sense of wonder. You might also feel admiration for the magician's skills. Perhaps you're irritated because you failed to figure out the trick. Emotions point us to the world: they concern a specific object or event that we attend to, such as the disappearance of the elephant, the clever magician, our own lack of knowledge. They include the subjective experience of an affect (internal feeling) such as wonder, and are frequently accompanied by behaviors: for example, our mouth may fall open, or we might exclaim, "Wow, where did it go?", in surprise or admiration. Inside our bodies, meanwhile, a complex cascade of neural and endocrinal changes happens. The brain areas involved in working memory and intentional gestures, for instance, show a heightened response as you watch the magician's actions.

Emotions and Biological Agency

The standard evolutionary picture of emotions, which many psychologists adhere to, broadly says that the function of emotions is to help organisms thrive, flourish, take care of their offspring, and avoid situations that cause them injury or death. This functional explanation fits within a bigger evolutionary account, namely of why organisms feel anything at all. Feeling and experience is widespread among living things.[4] For example, plants produce volatile organic chemicals in their leaves to counter infestation; they also use them to establish elaborate communicative networks with other plants.[5] They close and open their petals in response to the sun. It might be a stretch to call the trees in your back yard "conscious," but clearly responsiveness to the environment is biologically widespread, occurring in organisms that at first glance appear senseless. A basic awareness of the environment helps organisms act adaptively. As philosopher of biology Peter Godfrey-Smith puts it, "Nothing is gained biologically from taking in information that is not put to use. The evolution of the mind includes the coupled evolution of agency and subjectivity."[6] He sees the evolution of senses, including emotions, as fitting into this picture.

Emotions predispose us to behave in a certain way: for example, to flee (when afraid) or to fight (when angry or afraid). These reactions are not deterministic; rather they are *dispositions*. Emotions researcher Nico Frijda sees emotions as "relational action readiness."[7] A rabbit may be startled by your approach in the back yard, and prepares to flee: its ears become erect, the muscles in its powerful hind legs tense up. But it might also decide you don't pose an immediate threat and decide to keep nibbling the grass. This connection between outer stimuli to which we react and feelings that arise gives emotions their crucial role: they help us to be agents who can respond to our environment in flexible, adaptive ways. In this respect, they are a valuable source of information, just like perception, memory, reasoning, and our other faculties.

Tom Cochrane speculates that a key evolutionary innovation of emotions compared to other feelings such as pain is that they are more contextually oriented.[8] They are sensitive to possibility, to social context, to past experience. Pain is much less responsive to context than emotions typically are. For example, the rabbit in the back yard can become less afraid of you if it recognizes you or considers the time of day you tend to come out. Social censure might stop you from letting your anger at other motorists bloom into road rage. As a result of various selective pressures, the neural architecture of emotions differs across animal species. Humans and other primates, for instance, have four distinct neural areas which are involved in emotion-regulation: the brain stem, diencephalon, hippocampus, and orbitofrontal cortex.[9] All of these have developed as the result of distinct evolutionary trajectories and pressures, including social context, predation, and access to variable food sources.

Why is it useful to be responsive to context in our appraisals of the environment? The probable answer to this question is that it helps us to be more effective agents. The late evolutionary biologist Richard Lewontin (1929–2021) defended the idea that animals, plants, and other living things are not mere passive playthings of their environment, as the prevailing evolutionary picture for much of the twentieth century held. We should give proper place to agency in evolution.[10] An organism always interacts with its environment; it plays a role in its own fate. Each time a gazelle escapes a lion, through ingenuity and speed, it exerts (a very small, but still) selective pressure on lions to become better hunters of gazelles. Emotions, because they are so context-sensitive and non-deterministic, help animals to react appropriately to their environment and be effective agents.

The standard evolutionary picture of emotions in psychology and biology today owes much to Charles Darwin (1809–1882). Darwin applied his theory of natural selection to emotions in his *Expression of the Emotions in Man and Animals* (1872). Already in his *Descent of Man* (1871), he had speculated on the role of prosocial emotions in the evolution of human societies and morality. In *Expression of the Emotions,* he set the agenda for later scientific work on the emotions. The book stresses the continuity between human emotions and emotions in other animals. It looks at physiological markers of emotions, such as posture, vocal sounds, and especially facial expressions. Darwin identified precursors of human emotions such as surprise, sadness, fear, and joy in nonhuman animals, including monkeys and apes, cats, and dogs. He argued against his contemporaries who saw emotions as uniquely human and divinely inspired. He believed that our emotions are innate and adaptive, with only modest scope for cultural variation: human emotions as expressed through different cultures can be reduced to a relatively small set of core emotions, which have characteristic behaviors associated with them, notably facial expressions.

The psychologist Paul Ekman revived this Darwinian idea, hypothesizing that there is a small set of basic emotions, which "evolved for their adaptive value in dealing with *fundamental life tasks.*"[11] Ekman, like Darwin, associates the basic emotions with specific facial expressions. To identify them, he developed the Facial Action Coding System, which codes the facial muscle actions needed to express a given basic emotion. Ekman, Richard Sorenson, and Wallace Friesen examined how people from different cultures classified photos of facial expressions.[12] Even the Fore, a New Guinean group with almost no exposure to Western visual media at the time of the study, recognized a set of basic emotions, including anger, fear, happiness, sadness, disgust, and surprise that was modeled by American participants. More recent work on emotions also considers vocal expressions and body posture, such as clenching one's fists and shouting when angry.[13]

According to this standard picture, each basic emotion responds to a range of universal human predicaments. For example,

TABLE 1. Taxonomies of Basic Emotions

Izard	Panksepp	Ekman	Descartes
Happiness	Play	Happiness	Joy
Sadness	Sadness	Sadness	Sadness
Fear	Fear	Fear	
Anger	Rage	Anger	Hatred
Disgust		Disgust	
Contempt		Contempt	
	Lust		Desire
	Care		Love
Interest	Seeking	Surprise	Wonder

Partly based on Tracy and Randles, "Four models of basic emotions," Fig. 1 (p. 399)

the basic emotion of fear can be a response to fire, predators, or bullies. These basic emotions help us to behave appropriately under a range of conditions.[14] Fear helps us to escape dangerous situations, curiosity inspires us to seek out new sources of food or places of refuge, love helps us to bond with or care for offspring, friends, and partners. In social mammals such as primates, emotions have been subject to further selective pressure, to help them deal with socially complex situations.[15]

Psychologists and neuroscientists including Ekman, Carroll E. Izard, and Jaak Panksepp agree there is a limited set of basic emotions.[16] These basic emotions are discrete, associated with a fixed set of neural responses and bodily components. Most of these authors include at least one epistemic emotion in their list: either surprise, interest, or seeking. The evolutionary function of this basic epistemic emotion is to help us accommodate new information.

Table 1 gives an overview of basic emotions, as conceived by contemporary psychologists, and compares them to Descartes's taxonomy. Basic emotions are important building blocks;

however, they are not the only emotions that elicit expressions. Other emotions, such as embarrassment, pride, shame, and love, also elicit characteristic facial expressions, vocal responses, and bodily postures.[17] This has led some authors such as psychologist Lisa Feldman Barrett to develop alternative evolutionary accounts.[18] She thinks that we should not see emotions as "brute facts" or objective categories. Instead, humans culturally construct individual emotions from a set of more basic, psychologically primitive ingredients.

No matter what evolutionary framework we adopt, it needs to be able to answer the question of how humans seem able to have a rich, variable range of emotions beyond the basic ones we share with other animals. Social complexity might provide an answer: it is advantageous for socially complex and gregarious animals such as ourselves to be able to both discern and express subtle emotions such as pride, embarrassment, or gratitude. Even so, invoking selection through social evolution will not give us the full picture of emotional complexity we find across human cultures. Humans have a rich, nuanced, and sometimes culture-specific vocabulary for emotions.[19] When Portuguese speakers feel *saudade,* their emotion differs subtly from what German speakers call *Sehnsucht,* or Anglophones *nostalgia.*[20]

Let's look again at awe and wonder. As we saw, in Western philosophy these concepts were at first not differentiated from each other, as in *thauma* or *admiratio*. But later they became differentiated: for instance, in Adam Smith's two concepts of wonder and his distinction of wonder from both admiration and surprise. As history went on, awe and wonder acquired differing connotations. While awe was ambivalent or even negative (which is still clear in the word "awful," which used to mean the more neutral "awe-inspiring"), the concept of awe received a more positive valence in the early modern period, especially in the eighteenth-century literature by Edmund Burke, Immanuel Kant, and Johann Gottfried von Herder. Art played a crucial role in the positive re-evaluation of awe. Authors of gothic novels, such as Ann Radcliffe (1764–1823), helped us to value positively scenes of horror and danger.[21] These included steep mountain precipices, gloomy castles, and tempestuous seas, or being caught in a storm. You might experience the sublime directly when you were in actual danger, or vicariously through a novel or painting.

The question of how culture and cognition interact to give us a rich diversity of emotions is of enduring interest. While the standard Darwinian picture provides us with a plausible evolutionary basis for human emotions, it needs to be supplemented with an account of how culture interacts with our evolved cognitive architecture. I will show how we can manage and shape our emotions through cognitive technologies.

Shaping Our Emotions through Cognitive Technologies

Our emotions are not under our direct control, at least not on the spur of the moment. At the same time, we do many things that help us to regulate our emotions: we seek out the thrills of a rollercoaster ride, we visit a forest to soak in nature, we invite friends to enjoy the gentle flow of good conversation.

Mood-altering drugs, such as LSD and psilocybin can induce mystical experiences in their users, including a sense of oneness with one's environment or with the divine. They can induce a disintegration of the ordinary sense of self, feelings of awe and wonder, and a sense of boundless love. Based on a review of the recent empirical literature, Nin Kirkham and Chris

Letheby conclude that psychedelic drugs, through their long-lasting effects on our moods and emotions, can help us cultivate new virtues, including the virtue of being in harmony with our environment.[22]

We also scaffold our moods through art. We listen to music to modulate our emotions. Maybe you sometimes put a song on repeat: the music is no longer surprising to you, you know its modulations and rhythmic changes, but you put it on anyway because you know it makes you feel a certain way, and you crave to experience that feeling. Music has what Erik Rietveld calls "affective allure."[23] We are often irresistibly drawn to particular musical pieces in a powerful way. Music helps us to build up our emotions, like the scaffolding for a building. It helps us to regulate how we feel.[24] The way it does this is not always obvious. Take the use of sad music. Sad music is not *literally* sad. What you feel when listening to a sad piece is not so much sadness, as a kind of tenderness—a sweet and poignant feeling in the vicinity of compassion.[25] We might draw energy from music too, such as epic orchestral scores or techno. In the past, people had work songs such as sea-shanties. One of the longest-running popular music radio shows in the world is the Dutch *Arbeidsvitaminen* (literally, Work vitamins). When we feel fragmented and our moods and emotions are out of sorts, we revitalize ourselves and draw energy from music. We don't do this as isolated individuals. Music is often used in a group context: for instance, for religious ceremonies, as rousing political chants, or to express collective grief.

These are just a few examples of technologies that we use to alter our cognitive states. Historian Daniel Lord Smail refers to mood-altering institutions, behaviors, and practices such as taking drugs and listening to music as *psychotropic mechanisms*.[26] I see these as more specific instances of a general phenomenon, *cognitive technologies*. Unlike regular technologies such as those applied in ship-building or plumbing, that aim primarily to alter our physical environment, cognitive technologies aim to transform our cognitive environment, including what we know and what we feel about our surroundings.

Cognitive technologies need to be situated within a broader cognitive ecology. We often use material means, such as notebooks, pen-and-paper calculation, and, recently, smartphones and other electronic devices, to extend our cognition.[27] We can conceive of these as situated in cultural ecosystems that also embed our cognitive processes: our naked cognitive equipment (what goes on in our brain) is situated in a physical, embodied environment and interacts with that.[28]

Take the use of numerical notation systems, which allow us to denote quantities with much greater precision than we would be able to do purely verbally. When on a holiday, we quickly lose track of what day of the week it is. Our cognitive system is poorly equipped to keep track of even simple cyclical regularities such as the days of the week. A widespread cognitive technology such as a calendar allows us to keep track of events that occur cyclically, such as the seven days of the week, the phases of the moon, harvesting and planting systems. Calendars are ancient cognitive technologies, dating back at least thirty thousand years, as in the case of the Abri Blanchard bone (see chapter 1, 'Amateur Astronomy').[29] Cognitive technologies often involve physical props, such as a wall calendar or an abacus.

We can also use elaborate mental imaginings to enhance our cognition. In the chapters to follow, I'll apply this framework to the fields of magic, religion, and science and see how these harness our sense of awe and wonder. Here, I provide one particular example—Micronesian sea navigation—to give a general sense of how cognitive technologies work. Micronesian traditional sea navigation is detailed in Thomas Gladwin's seminal ethnographical study *East is a Big Bird* (1970).[30] Pacific navigators travel from small island to small island with traditional sailing canoes for trips that last (if the winds are favorable) two or three days:

> The canoe itself, a narrow V-shaped hull usually about 26 feet long, with platforms extending out both sides, lurches with a violence which requires constant holding on. If the crew is lucky and the wind holds steady, this pitching and twisting will go on without rest day and night for the day or two or three it takes to reach their destination. But the wind may drop and leave the crew drifting or dawdling along under an equatorial sun. Or it may rise to a storm with gusts wracking the canoe and driving chilling rain into the skin and eyes of the crew. Through all of this the navigator, in sole command, keeps track of course and drift and position, guided only by stars and waves and other signs of the sea, and in recent years by a large but unlighted compass. Even at night he stays awake and vigilant, trusting only himself. They say you can tell the experienced navigators by their bloodshot eyes.[31]

How is the navigator able to reach his destination, if all he can see for miles around is the unruly ocean and the endless blue expanse? Micronesian navigators use multiple cues, such as reefs, flocks of fish, birds, and especially the setting and rising of stars on the horizon. In these regions near the equator, stars appear to travel vertically across the sky, appearing and disappearing at set points during the night. Every navigator has within his mind a star compass. He has learned it painstakingly, through diagrams of pebbles, representing the stars, placed in a circle—the canoe is in the middle of the circle, and is conceived of as stationary, while the stars are conceptualized as traveling. An aspiring navigator needs to learn the trajectory of stars for trips between known islands. The training is only complete if he "at his instructor's request can start with any island in the known ocean and rattle off the stars both going and returning between that island and all the others which might conceivably be reached directly from there."[32] The Micronesian star compass is a cognitive technology that uses the environment (the positioning of stars near the equator) and human memory, as well as an elaborate instructional context with sets of pebbles and rote recitation.

Beyond Nature and Nurture: How Emotions are Scaffolded

Just as we can improve performance of cognitive tasks such as time-keeping or navigation through cognitive technologies, we can improve and modify our emotions and moods.[33] As we've seen, we can use psychotropic drugs and music to do this. We can also use other aspects of our physical environment to alter our emotions. For example, religious buildings are often shaped to facilitate a sense of awe: they are tall and imposing, with stained glass windows filtering the light in a specific way. Worshippers synchronize voices and movements in rituals, creating a feeling of togetherness.[34]

Starting out from the standard Darwinian picture, we can appreciate that emotions help us make adaptive decisions. They help us to be successful agents in the world; they are products of evolution. But emotions are also culturally variable. We can invoke cognitive technologies to help explain how this cultural variation occurs. Psychologist Celia Heyes discusses cognitive technologies (or "cognitive gadgets," as she calls them) that we deploy in a range of situations, such as when we rely on theory of mind.[35] Theory of mind is cross-culturally universal: we predict what other people will say and do by inferring their mental states. However, there is significant cultural variation: for example, in the extent to which we attribute motives to someone's inner drive, or to their broader environment. Several studies indicate that East Asians tend to see people's actions as influenced by their surroundings, whereas Westerners (particularly Americans) tend to see their actions more as a result of individual characteristics and decisions.[36]

In Heyes's view, theory of mind has both innate and cultural components. Everything we do is suffused with both nature and nurture, but the biological and cultural components can be distinguished. For example, walking is deeply instinctual, as we can see in the reflexes of a newborn baby, but there is cultural influence upon how we saunter, stroll, or amble. Nevertheless, Heyes deems it methodologically important to pinpoint the contributions of evolved capacities and culturally inherited ideas and beliefs in our behavior. To what extent does biology constrain our cultural expression? Precise details for any given instance depend on both good conceptual tools and empirical work, and this is also true for awe and wonder. A comprehensive study of how awe and wonder are expressed in different cultures, or across time within a given culture, would require significant cross-cultural work, which has only recently been undertaken.[37]

From this general theoretical picture, it follows that emotions are, on the one hand, scaffolded by the (social and natural) environment and, on the other, both natural and evolved. The standard picture of a few basic emotions needs to be supplemented by an account of how we use our cultural tools to scaffold our emotions and to elaborate them, as well as socially share them.[38] For example, in Arabic *tarab* denotes a musically induced state of ecstasy. Social sharing of emotions allows us to express not only the basic emotions we have in common with other mammals, but also the more sophisticated emotions involved in pleasurable human pursuits such as philosophy, science, and music.

Art and other products of human culture play an important role in this emotional scaffolding. Works of art don't simply slot into a pre-set number of emotional receptors, as Steven Pinker argued when he proposed that art's primary function is to "press our pleasure buttons."[39] In his evolutionary-psychological account of the mind, Pinker endorses a strong nativist, modular view of human cognition. He thinks the mind has a large set of pre-set, evolved cognitive dispositions or modules which respond to the environment in a predictable way. He likens the gratification we sense when we consume art to eating cheesecake. Cheesecake is not particularly healthy or good for us, but it satisfies our ancient, once-adaptive cravings for sugar and fat. An obvious problem with this account is how to explain food that is not like cheesecake, or art that challenges rather than gratifies. A lot of great art, such as Francisco Goya's gloomy political canvases or Egon Schiele's bleak and unsexy nudes, is hardly eye candy, but on the contrary disquieting.[40]

Art helps to shape and alter our tastes. To continue the culinary analogy, we enjoy cheesecake, but many other culinary delights besides, including the bitterness of chicory endives, and the unapologetically pungent complexity of durian. Though we all have a limited set of gustatory and olfactory receptors, our cognitive appreciation of what we taste and smell is scaffolded by our environment. The chapters that follow will discuss magic, religion, and science as cognitive technologies that help us to kindle a sense of awe and wonder. First, however, let's look in a bit more detail at psychological work on awe and wonder, to get a better grasp on what kinds of emotions we are dealing with.

The Psychology of Awe

The psychology of awe has enjoyed renewed attention thanks to a landmark paper by psychologists Dacher Keltner and Jonathan Haidt.[41] In their view, awe has two key components: it is elicited by a *perception of vastness*, which prompts a *need for accommodation*. Vastness can mean large physical size. Standing in a grove of tall trees, or on top of a high tower, or even sitting beneath a life-size replica of a *Tyrannosauros rex* skeleton, reliably elicit awe.[42] Vastness can also be conceptual: a complex and all-encompassing scientific theory such as evolutionary theory or quantum mechanics, an imposing musical composition such as J. S. Bach's B-minor mass, or a rich secondary world such as J.R.R. Tolkien's Middle Earth can leave us awestruck.[43] Actions with vast ramifications can likewise elicit awe. For example, the demolition of the Berlin Wall was awe-inspiring for those who witnessed it, not because of the smashing of the concrete barriers, but because it symbolized the unification of a fractured Germany.

Although Keltner and Haidt originally conceptualized awe as rare and fleeting, experienced mainly at life-changing moments such as childbirth, more recent research indicates that, at least according to self-reports, awe is an emotion we experience frequently. Diary studies suggest people sense awe about twice or thrice a week. Many things can elicit awe, even a walk in a local park or watching a sports event on television.[44] Since then Keltner,[45] and others, have documented that awe is frequent and that it isn't reserved to people who have wealth or leisure. People living in poverty, prisons, and other difficult circumstances also frequently experience moments of awe.

The second core component of awe is a need for accommodation. We feel a need for accommodation when the vastness we experience doesn't fit into our pre-existing conceptual schemas. This leads to a perception of a gap in our knowledge. Awe has both a social and an epistemic dimension. In social terms, awe modulates how we perceive our relationship to others. Empirical studies have demonstrated that awe elicits a sense of "small self"—it makes us humbler.[46] For example, Paul K. Piff and colleagues placed participants in a grove of towering and majestic eucalyptus trees (the awe condition), or asked them to look up at a tall, plain-looking university building (the control condition).[47] Participants who had stood among the trees responded significantly less self-entitledly, choosing smaller rewards for their participation in the study. Awe also makes people feel more connected and at one with their environment. The vastness of space gives rise to an "overview effect," whereby individuals see themselves as part of a bigger whole. An extreme but clear example can be seen in self-reports of astronauts: contemplating the vastness of space elicits awe and facilitates a sense of oneness with humanity and the cosmos. The self shrinks to be part of a bigger whole. Under experimental conditions, awe is associated with an alteration of one's self-concept and increased identification with universal statements, such as that one is a living being or part of humanity.[48]

In epistemic terms, awe's close connection to knowledge deserves scrutiny. Since awe prompts a need for accommodation, it encourages us to revise and perhaps even abandon our schemas. (In chapter 6 I will examine how this makes awe an important emotion for scientific practice.) In our everyday lives, we use schemas (such as stereotypes, heuristics, scripts) to make sense of what happens around us. For example, a classic paper by Amos Tversky and Daniel Kahneman describes a series of heuristics, principles that people use to reduce the complex task of making probability judgments.[49] One of these is availability: to assess how likely an event is, such as a heart attack in middle-age, you try to recall if you know people within this category. If you can readily recall a few examples of middle-aged people who had heart attacks, you will deem this event more likely. Stereotypes about race, gender, and other categories are used to make quick judgments and decisions, leading, for example, to fewer callbacks for job applicants with African American-sounding names. Positive moods and emotions, such as joy and amusement, tend to make us think more creatively, globally, and flexibly, but they also make us more reliant on schemas, which causes us to overlook details and renders us vulnerable to weak argumentation. By contrast, negative moods and emotions, such as sadness, encourage attention to detail and critical thinking.[50] The evolutionary rationale behind this is that emotions provide us with information. A positive emotion entices us to continue what we are doing and to take advantage of a situation. A negative emotion encourages us to drop our usual way of thinking and to carefully reappraise our situation.[51] This explains why advertisements want to make us laugh and feel happy—you become less critical when you're happy.

An exception to this robust pattern, however, is awe. Awe can be either positive—when you view something beautiful and inspiring—or negative—for instance, during spring 2020, when people saw hospitalizations and deaths from Covid-19 rise very quickly.[52] Awe reduces people's reliance on schemas and makes them more open-minded. At the same time, it enhances critical thinking. Several studies that induced awe in participants found that people tend to think more critically in the awe condition compared to a neutral condition.[53] For example, they are better able to spot the weaknesses in an argument. This empirical research (which is still rapidly expanding at the time of writing) indicates that awe is a self-transcendent and epistemic emotion. In social terms, it helps us to transcend a focus on the self and see ourselves instead as part of an interconnected whole. In epistemic terms, it leads us to question what we think we know and encourages us to change our mind and be more investigative. In order to regulate our lives, both are important for us.

Most contemporary work on awe dates to the last two decades, but it builds on older work on the sublime in philosophy of art and aesthetics. It is worth discussing this literature in some detail here, as the psychological work on awe is clearly inspired by these earlier writings. The sublime is a major component of aesthetic value, alongside the beautiful. Discussions on the sublime were prominent in the eighteenth century, with contributions by authors such as Edmund Burke (1729–1797), Immanuel Kant (1724–1804), and Johann Gottfried von Herder (1744–1803). Many sublime objects are deemed beautiful, such as sunrises, the ocean, or the starry night sky. According to these early theorists, whereas beautiful things are often symmetrical, sublime things have an element of wildness or disorder. A jagged mountain ridge can be sublime without being beautiful.[54] Burke saw astonishment as the emotional basis of the sense of the sublime.[55] He thought the sublime was ambivalent, closer to pain than to pleasure. This contrasts with beauty, associated solely with pleasure. The sublime seems just too vast to be mentally accommodated. Burke conceptualized awe (in his terminology, "astonishment") as closely related to terror. Astonishment, admiration, reverence, and respect are related—Burke conceived of these emotions as graded, with astonishment being the strongest and gradually diminishing in strength to respect.

According to these eighteenth-century authors, the primary elicitor of the sublime is vastness. This close similarity between awe and the sublime has led philosopher Robert Clewis to propose that the sublime is in fact a kind of awe: namely, aesthetic awe.[56] A further element of the sublime, but more contested than vastness, is lack of knowledge. Kant's account of the sublime incorporates an inability to comprehend; once we understand something, we no longer judge it to be sublime.[57] By contrast, his contemporary Herder did not deem lack of understanding to be a core of the sublime. In his untranslated *Kalligone* (1800) Herder criticized the Kantian account.[58] He observed that people at the time he was writing knew far more about the starry heavens above than did people in antiquity. Moreover, they had some understanding of the laws that govern their motions; yet they found the heavens even more impressive than before. We got a sense of this early modern sublime of the cosmos in the previous chapter, when we discussed early popularizing works by Fontenelle and others. Thus, while vastness has been a standard feature of accounts of awe and the sublime, there is disagreement on the extent to which a lack of understanding contributes to its aesthetic appeal.

Like awe, the sublime is associated with both self-negation and elevation. Self-negation is an annihilation of the sense of self-importance. In Tom Cochrane's view, there are two routes in Kant's philosophy by which we can arrive at this self-negation: by being violently impacted upon (for instance, by viewing extreme natural phenomena), or by being confronted by concepts or theories of great profundity for the first time.[59] But it is possible to feel both elevated *and* diminished: for instance, when confronted with imagery of distant galaxies from the Webb telescope. In Kant's *Critique of Practical Reason* (1788), we see an emphasis on the self-elevation aspect of awe, notably in this famous concluding passage:

> Two things fill the mind with ever new and increasing admiration and reverence, the more frequently and persistently one's meditation deals with them: *the starry sky above me and the moral law within me.*[60]

Kant argued that both starry sky and morality elicit a sense of the sublime because of their impact on how he perceived himself. When he looked at the sky on a clear night, he did not just see a pretty and scenic sight. In his *Universal Natural History and Theory of the Heavens* (1755), he had developed an elaborate theory of cosmic evolution that was centuries ahead of its time, wherein he identified the distant nebulae that could be viewed with a telescope as galaxies, similar to the Milky Way. Even as late as the 1920s, astronomers were debating whether there were multiple galaxies. Kant hypothesized in 1755 that telescopes were too weak to detect that these faraway galaxies were in fact composed of stars. Scaling up in a dizzying way, he speculated that galaxies could be part of even larger systems:

> If the magnitude of a planetary system in which the Earth is as a grain of sand and scarcely noticeable puts our reason into a state of wonderment, then with what amazement are we delighted when we contemplate the infinite multitude of worlds and systems that constitute the sum total of the Milky Way; but how much does this amazement increase when one becomes aware that all these immeasurable orders of stars in turn are the unit of a number whose end we do not know.[61]

He also considered deep time, speculating that

> [c]reation is not the work of one moment [. . .]. Millions and whole mountain ranges of millions of centuries will pass within which ever new worlds and world-orders will form and attain completion one after another in the remote distances from the center point of nature."[62]

So when Kant considers the starry sky over three decades later in *Critique of Practical Reason,* he says it "expands the connection in which I stand into the immensely large, with worlds upon worlds and systems of systems [galaxy clusters], and also into boundless times of their periodic motion, the beginning and continuance thereof."[63] He finds the starry sky daunting:

> a countless multitude of worlds, which annihilates, as it were, my importance as an *animal creature* that, after having for a short time been provided (one knows not how) with vital force, must give back again to the planet (a mere dot in the universe) the matter from which it came.[64]

In contrast to his perception of the stars, Kant's sense of the moral law starts within himself and "elevates infinitely my worth as that of an *intelligence* by my personality, in which the moral law reveals to me a life independent of animality [. . .] that is not restricted to conditions and boundaries of this life but proceeds to infinity."[65] In the contemporary literature, the two elicitors Kant described are associated with two distinct emotions: awe for the starry sky, and *elevation* for the moral law within. Elevation, or moral elevation, shares some features with awe. It tends to be elicited when we witness virtuous actions by others. Phenomenologically, it is often accompanied by a sense of warmth, but unlike awe, it does not require vastness.[66]

Within the psychological literature, authors discuss whether awe is a basic emotion, and if so, what its evolutionary function might be. Keltner and Haidt, and Michelle Shiota and colleagues, see awe as basic.[67] However, awe is also complex and multifaceted. As Keltner and Haidt define it, awe can be "flavored" with, among other elements, fear (when we see a tornado approach), beauty (when we view a majestic waterfall at a safe distance), or admiration (when we see someone perform an exceptional feat, such as a difficult jump by a gymnast or a high aria by a coloratura soprano). This complexity speaks against awe being a basic emotion.

An emotion need not be basic to be adaptive. Indeed, as Keltner and colleagues argue, complex emotions also help us to engage with the world, and a complex social environment requires complex emotions as well as an ability to recognize such emotions in ourselves and others.[68] Awe helps us to regulate our social interactions and our sense of self. Beyond this, it is epistemic, allowing us to appraise and question what we think we know. Due to our engagement with art, religion, science, and other cultural elements, we can expand our engagement with awe and the scope of things we feel awe at. It is adaptive for us to regulate our social interactions and understand our situation within a group, and to understand that we lack certain knowledge about the world. We continuously expand our sense of awe to incorporate new objects and features of the environment, which is useful for creatures like us. After all, hominins have lived in constantly changing surroundings since at least five million years ago. When you live in variable environments, it is not useful for emotions to be too tightly responsive to a fixed set of stimuli.[69] By cultivating appropriate emotional responses to our evolving world, we can become more effective agents. As I will argue in the chapters that follow, the cases of magic, religion, and science show how we can harness our emotions to engage with the world. Awe plays a crucial role in these cognitive technologies, as does wonder.

The Psychology of Wonder

In the psychological literature, wonder has not received as much attention as awe. For one thing, it is not always clearly differentiated from awe. For example, Keltner and Piff write that "awe creates the mental state of wonder, which leads to the search for knowledge, a recognition of one's position within the broader social context, and prosocial inclination."[70] Thus, it seems that for them, wonder is not an emotion but a broader mental state *caused* by the emotion of awe. In his seminal study of the emotions, Frijda links wonder to surprise and amazement, and describes it as a passive, receptive form of attention that we have when we experience something unexpected.[71] This is very much in line with the philosophical tradition on wonder, as we saw in the previous chapter.

Yet, there is a small body of empirical and conceptual work that indicates that awe and wonder are distinct emotions. As we will see in the next chapter, a lot of this work focuses on stage magic, an art form that is specifically meant to elicit wonder in the audience, so I will defer discussion of the magic-related literature to chapter 4. A word frequency study that compared people's free word associations to wonder, awe, and happiness helps to bring out some differences between awe and wonder: compared to awe, wonder elicits fewer positive emotion words (e.g., "love") and fewer anxiety words (e.g., "worried").[72] Awe links to more first-person plural pronouns (we, our, us), in line with its social dimension and its ability to achieve a sense of oneness with others and the environment. However, awe is also associated with fewer insight words (such as "think") and causation words (e.g., "because") than wonder, and fewer tentative words (e.g., "perhaps"). This is consistent with wonder being a primarily epistemic emotion, with perhaps less of a social dimension than awe.

Psychologist Michelle "Lani" Shiota describes the phenomenology of wonder as follows:

> We are aware of some gaps—those that lie at the fringes of our current understanding. When the topic is important to us, this awareness of gaps leads to wonder—the desire to know more. Wonder is highly motivating; the search for knowledge is experienced as fun, and the sense of reward that comes from acquiring new knowledge is great.[73]

In other words, wonder is a distinct and independent emotion. Based on the limited empirical literature and philosophical work, I have phrased my working definition of wonder that is partly based on this, which we saw in chapter 1:

> wonder is the emotion that arises when we are confronted with gaps in our knowledge. It arises from a glimpse at the unknown terrain which lies just beyond the fringes of our current understanding. Like awe, it prompts a need for cognitive accommodation, but it does not necessarily have the dimension of vastness.

At present, I think our best guess is that neither awe nor wonder are basic emotions; but that doesn't mean they are not evolutionarily significant. Biologically, they are significant because they help us to be more effective agents. They clearly have epistemic as well as social dimensions that matter from an evolutionary point of view. It is useful for limited, time-bound and space-bound organisms to be able to let go of heuristics and schemas that apparently don't work. Awe and wonder accomplish this by alerting us to new information and making us more aware of our cognitive limitations. Moreover, these evolved responses have become elaborated by various cultural means including cognitive technologies. In the chapters that follow, we will see how magic, religion, and science draw on awe and wonder.

4

Wonder and the Origins of Magic

Magic: The Most Sacred Philosophy

Magical ability possesses great power, full of the highest mysteries, contemplating profound secret things, natures, power, qualities, substances, and virtues, combined with the understanding of all of nature. It instructs us on how things are different from each

> other and how they agree. Wonderful effects are produced from magic, uniting virtues by applying things with each other and by accepting their congruity, and everywhere binds and marries inferior and superior gifts and virtues. This is the most perfect and highest science, the highest and most sacred philosophy.
>
> —HEINRICH CORNELIUS AGRIPPA[1]

You watch a magic show. The magician tosses coins into a water tank. By a wave of his hand, they turn into goldfish. You experience a sense of wonder, caused by the impossibility of this feat: it's impossible that coins turn into fish, yet this is what happens. How did he do it? Although you know there must be a trick to it, your sense of wonder does not disappear. As a performance art, magic encourages our sense of wonder.[2]

Judging by subreddits, Discord servers, and YouTube channels, interest in hermeticism, magic, and alchemy has recently surged. Yet, magic—as a human practice—has not received much attention in academic philosophy. A few centuries ago, this was very different. The German polymath Heinrich Cornelius Agrippa (1486–1535) called magic the "highest and most sacred philosophy," and he was not alone in this idea. Other Renaissance and early modern philosophers, such as Marsilio Ficino (1433–1499), Giovanni Pico della Mirandola (1463–1494), and Giordano Bruno (1548–1600), likewise believed that magic is central to our endeavors to know more about the world. While their humanism has received a lot of attention, their interest in magic now strikes us as odd. Only recently, philosophers have begun to investigate the Renaissance interest in magic.[3]

Why aren't contemporary philosophers more interested in magic? It may be due to its close association with superstition, stage performance, and perhaps also its unabashed and open reliance on trickery and deception. Still, the enormous successes of fantasy fiction, TV shows, and table top games, the enduring appeal of magical practices such as tarot and astrology, as well as of stage magic, indicate that magic appeals to something deep within us. As practicing stage magician and philosopher Lawrence Hass notes, the practice of magic responds to our need to experience wonder, and to experience wonder is an integral part of a well-lived life: "As a longtime performer, I can attest to the fact that most people find excellent performance magic ecstatic: transporting, pleasurable, and sublime."[4] Without a little magic in our lives, without a place for the unexpected and the wondrous, life is dull and drab.

The term "magic" in its contemporary sense covers several distinct, yet related ideas, and I aim to be broad in my treatment of the theme. I will cover magic in genre fantasy, and stage magic, as well as practices relating to the occult. While these three senses of magic are distinct, it makes sense to treat them together, as it is hard to make principled distinctions between "real" and "pretend" magic, given how historically these two have consistently been intermingled.[5] When, for instance, shamans and other magical practitioners perform their art, they make frequent use of stage magic techniques such as forcing, sleight of hand, and mental suggestion.

Wonder is the unifying thread in these seemingly disparate senses of magic. I provide the following working definition for what I mean by "magic" in this chapter and later in the book. This is not meant as a definitive summation of magic, but rather as a useful guide to unify the different contexts in which magic is evoked or practiced:

> Magic is the collective term for human practices that harness a perceived, intended, or feigned ability to produce wonders.

This working definition draws our attention to two aspects of magic: respectively, its active power and its passive receptivity for wonder. *Magic as power* is being able to do things that are deemed impossible. *Magic as wonder* is our ability to feel moved and astounded by things we deem impossible. These two features have been at the core of magic for a long time: the etymology of the English word "magic" relates to the Proto-Indo-European for "power." The English term derives from the ancient Greek *mageia*, whose modern vernacular descendants are words such as *magia* (Spanish) and *magie* (Dutch). The word "thaumaturgy" has the Greek root *thaumazein*, which, as we have seen, means "to wonder." In the early modern period, there was a consensus that the practice of magic concerned itself with wonders.

In this chapter, I examine how magic harnesses our sense of wonder, looking at the use of magic in genre fantasy, stage magic, and magical practice. Genre fantasy helps us to see that there are two aspects to magic: magic as a way to accomplish something, and magic as a way to experience something. I then consider stage magic. We will see how stage magic sheds light on the human emotion of wonder. I propose that stage magic is an art form which has as its main purpose to evoke wonder in the audience. Finally, I look at magical practices that aim to change the world, with an examination of the cognitive science of magic and a brief history of magical practices in Western culture. This examination of magic reveals intriguing continuities with science, leading us to ask whether and how there might be continuity from older, magical practices to the scientific revolution. I'll look at attempts to trace the historical roots of science in magic, and then indicate how wonder unifies both practices.

Hard and Soft Magic

John Clute and John Grant's *Encyclopedia of Fantasy* (1997) notes in its entry on "Magic" that there is a remarkable consensus on what magic is among contemporary writers of genre fantasy fiction. Magic is boundless in its possibilities, capable of anything a writer could conceive. However, within the fantasy story, it has to obey certain rules. It is a practice that widens our possibilities and expands what readers can conceive of as physically possible, but it is also subject to its own constraints. In genre fantasy fiction, these help to ensure that magic does not destroy the plot. Without being subject to constraints, the conflict that characters experience, and that is so integral to plot, would melt away.

The fantasy author Brandon Sanderson makes a distinction between *hard* and *soft* magic. When Sanderson started out writing, he believed—like many other fantasy writers—that the main thing to consider when inventing a magic system is to introduce internally consistent rules for that magic in a clear and expository manner. To craft a fantasy world is to create a world with alternative laws of nature. We can see this clearly in Sanderson's own work, such as *Mistborn*, a trilogy of epic fantasy novels with meticulously explained magical systems. For example, in *The Hero of Ages*, the third book of the series, we read,

> Vin burned electrum. This created a cloud of images around her, shadows of possible things she could do in the future. Electrum, the Allomantic complement of gold. Elend had started calling it "poor man's atium." It wouldn't affect the battle much, other than to make her immune to atium, should the Inquisitor have any.[6]

In the *Mistborn* trilogy, magic users burn various metals in their bodies. Each metal gives users a different magical ability. In this case, electrum gives a range of possible futures as separate images. Gold shows them possible pasts that never happened. Atium allows one to anticipate the moves of an opponent by seeing a few moments into their future course of action.

When Sanderson discussed his insight into magic at a panel at WorldCon, a large annual fantasy and SF convention, he found to his surprise that many panelists disagreed with him. They said, "If you have lots of rules and boundaries for your magic [. . .] you lose your sense of wonder! Fantasy is all about wonder! You can't restrict yourself, or your imagination, by making your magic have rules!"[7] This led Sanderson to draw a distinction between hard magic, which is rule-based, and soft magic, which is meant to elicit a sense of wonder and mystery. Soft magic does not reveal its rules explicitly. Sanderson believes soft magic also has rules, but these remain implicit and are not explained to the reader. The two kinds of magic lie along a continuum and often appear together in one work.

I want to explore another difference between hard and soft magic: hard magic emphasizes magic as power, and soft magic emphasizes the wondrousness of magic. In stories where hard magic prevails, the magic is like a technology. It has clear purposes and achieves clear ends, as in Ursula Le Guin's *Earthsea* book series.[8] In stories where soft magic is central, magic is wondrous and without clear purposes or ends, as in the powers of the unicorn that remain mysterious in Peter S. Beagle's *Last Unicorn*. The two main wizards (*Istari*) in Tolkien's *Lord of the Rings* provide a useful illustration of this contrast between hard and soft magic. Saruman and his industrialized Isengard represent hard magic. He uses magic for purely utilitarian ends. Gandalf represents soft magic. He is a mysterious figure, uncanny, unfathomable, who comes and goes, and baffles the reader as much as he baffles hobbits and dwarves in the story. We never quite fully grasp how he came back from his battle with the Balrog, what his deal is with the eagles, or how his magic works. His is the second kind of magic, magic as wonder.

In fantasy literature, the two kinds of magic interact dynamically. Any world with a magical system evokes a sense of wonder in us, as well as a vicarious sense of power and control. For example, the idea that you too could be enrolled into a magic school and find yourself exploring your hidden powers (a common plot device in children's fantasy) is irresistible.[9] These two elements of power and wonder are also present in stage magic. In the next section, I focus on the practice of stage magic to better assess this connection between wonder and power. Stage magic makes a useful case study, because it has been a recent object of scrutiny in cognitive psychology and neuroscience. Indeed, the most extensive research on wonder and the kinds of stimuli that elicit it concerns stage magic.

Stage Magic as Wonder-Technology

Stage magic is a universal human performing art. It is both ancient and ubiquitous. For example, in Exodus (the second book of the Hebrew Bible, ca. sixth century BCE), Pharaoh does not want to release the enslaved Israelites, because the feat that Moses and Aaron perform, turning a staff into a live snake, is something his court magicians can also accomplish (Exodus 7:10–12; if there is a historical basis to this story, presumably the court magicians were able to perform basic stage magic tricks, leading the Pharaoh to believe Moses and Aaron did not work a true miracle). Stage magic is also a reflective, deeply philosophical practice. As characterized by prominent practitioners Penn and Teller, stage magic is about "exploring epistemology"; it is "the heaviest philosophical ideas you can possibly have, dealt with in the silliest way," particularly because misbelief does not have dire consequences. When done well, "it brings out a huge amount of wonder."[10]

Stage magic appeals to our sense of wonder. When we watch a magical performance, we have a peculiar experience, which arises out of a cognitive tension between our expectation that "x cannot happen" and our perception that "x happens."[11] It is impossible that lifeless coins tossed into an aquarium should turn into live goldfish, and yet this is what we see. It is impossible for the magician Derren Brown to transfer telepathically the suit and rank of a playing card into the minds of his audience. And yet, seemingly, that's what he does.

What makes stage magic feel magical is a combination of several elements. There is the teleology of the action (the story that underlies the stage performance), the effect of impossibility achieved through natural means, and the sense of wonder in the spectator. Non-practitioners often assume that what lies at the basis of a magic performance is a single secret, often the moment when a sleight of hand is supposed to happen. However, a successful total performance requires much more than this: setting an appropriate mood, finding poetry and beauty with a limited set of props and in a short timeframe—these are just as important, if not more so.[12] For example, in Silverfish, the trick whereby coins turn into goldfish, Teller plays with our strong intuitive expectations that lifeless objects cannot turn into live animals. It is more wondrous to have something lifeless become alive than the other way around. This observation is confirmed in numerous cognitive science experiments, as Pascal Boyer has shown.[13] According to Boyer, violations of what he terms our "ontological expectations" create a sense of wonder and engrain themselves in our memory: shoes that sprout roots, or humans turning into animals (or the other way around) are particularly memorable. Violations within schemas can also be memorable; for example, we would not expect sheep to be carnivorous. Anything odd and wondrous will stick in our minds.[14]

For this reason, it is also misleading to say that magicians fool or trick their audience (excepting those who try to make their audience believe they truly have special powers—for instance, in scamming attempts to allegedly bring people into contact with deceased loved ones). It is more accurate to say that magicians achieve an effect of impossibility, making spectators experience something they deem impossible, thereby eliciting a sense of wonder. To evoke wonder, magicians must implicitly know a great deal about the human mind. Sleight of hand is only one—and often a relatively minor—component of the magician's skillset.[15]

Since most of the audience must feel the effect of impossibility, magic must exploit stable features of human cognition. To adopt an insight from vision scientist Patrick Cavanagh: a magical performance is in some sense a discovery of neuroscience, because for the trick to work, it must home in on the limitations and possibilities of the way the human mind works.[16] Cavanagh observed that a painter doesn't need to be realistic in their representation of shadows, because the human mind doesn't really care about shadows, and thus can tap into a simplified physics with which the brain deals with the world. Similarly, a magician can use misdirection techniques to focus attention on the hand that is supposed to produce the coins (in the Miser's Dream trick), while the other hand is meanwhile actually doing so. The misdirection that produces the illusion must be robust across the audience. For this reason, cognitive scientists can use magic as a framework to study the mind.[17] Magic exploits a wide range of cognitive limitations, such as our reliance on testimony (e.g., we tend to believe what a hapless audience member says), and the way we process visual, auditory, and other sensory information.

Take the cups and balls, a widespread piece of performance magic that was already mentioned by Seneca in the first century CE,[18] and that is performed across the world, including in India and Japan. A ball seemingly vanishes from the closed fist of the magician to magically reappear under one of three cups. This performance relies on object permanence and on our strong propensity to assign intentionality to hand gestures. If a ball is seemingly transferred from one hand to another, we tend to perceive that it actually happens. The magician uses misdirection (demonstrating that one of the cups is empty) to maneuver the ball. After habituating the audience to several balls appearing under cups, the trick often culminates in a much larger object, such as a lemon or tennis ball, appearing from under the remaining cup. The astonishment the audience feels relies on a well-established psychological technique, namely habituation. By the end of the performance, the audience has formed the expectation that balls of the same size appear under the cups. Then, that expectation is violated when a lemon or tennis ball appears. Applause.

Another common technique, especially prominent in card magic, is "forcing." Forcing is the method of controlling a choice made by a spectator during a performance. To achieve this, a magician might use physical positioning and verbal and nonverbal primes to compel a spectator to make a predetermined choice while giving the illusion of total freedom.[19] As Gustav Kuhn and colleagues describe it, such techniques are "forcing you to experience wonder," through the cognitive dissonance experienced between the feeling of free choice and a predetermined outcome. For example, if presented with a line of five cards and asked to pick one at random, very few people will choose the first or last card (edge avoidance). People are not good at randomizing their own behavior, and perceive the choice of the first or last card as non-random. As they will probably not pick the middle card either, the volunteer will very likely choose the second or fourth card. Magicians rely on these stable features of human cognition to constrain choice.

In performance magic, surprise and wonder come apart in the way Adam Smith hypothesized (see chapter 2). As spectators, we fully expect the magician will guess our card, but because we do not know how it is done we "will still wonder, though forewarned of what we are to see," as Smith describes wonder.[20] Though experiences in stage magic can be flavored with surprise or admiration, the core affect is wonder, and specifically Smith's second kind of wonder, which

> arises from an unusual succession of things. The stop which is thereby given to the career of the imagination, the difficulty which it finds in passing along such disjointed objects, and the feeling of something like a gap or interval betwixt them, constitute the whole essence of this emotion.[21]

This dissociation between wonder and surprise occurs at the neural level. In one neuroimaging (fMRI) study, participants were shown three versions of the same event: (1) the magic condition, a classic coin disappearance trick in which a magician covers a coin with his hand, and the coin vanishes; (2) a control condition, where the coin was still there; and (3) a surprise condition, where another hand swipes in unexpectedly to snatch the coin away. Compared to the other conditions, the magic condition revealed significantly greater activations in left DLPFC or dorsolateral prefrontal cortex (BA46), right dorsomedial PFC (BA9), right DLPFC (BA10), right precuneus (BA19), and further areas in the parietal lobe bilaterally (BA40).[22] While the other brain areas are mainly involved in spatial cognition, the left DLPFC is involved when we direct our attention, and perform voluntary action, and retain things in working memory. What we see at the neural level is the brain trying to figure out what happened to the coin (it should still be there, as working memory tells us it is there). We encode that somebody intentionally made it disappear. This generates a sense of wonder.

As I suggested earlier, stage magic keys into *human* cognitive dispositions. For this reason, we might expect that members of other species are not fooled by some of the tricks that are compelling to humans. This is indeed the case for Eurasian jays (*Garrulus glandarius*). These birds, like other corvids, cache their food and are sometimes victims of others pilfering their caches. They rely on sleight of beak to deceive each other, such as pretending to cache food at one location when they're in the presence of a conspecific, only to surreptitiously seek out another spot when the other looks away. Elias Garcia-Pelegrin and colleagues offered jays the choice between two closed hands for a reward.[23] The birds were not fooled by French drop or palm transfer, and chose the correct hand the majority of times (over seventy percent). The French drop is a classic technique whereby an object seems to be transferred, while remaining in its original position. In spite of its ubiquity and classic status in stage magic, humans continue to be fooled by it. This was also the case for this experiment: unlike jays, humans picked the wrong hand approximately seventy-five percent of times in the French drop condition, compared to a control. However, like humans, Eurasian jays are fooled by speedy transfers between hands.

The neuroscience and psychology of stage magic indicate that magic harnesses human cognitive dispositions to force us to experience wonder. When we go to a magic show, we go in with the expectation of seeing the impossible, but we also realize that what we will witness are mere illusions. What then, about magicians who purport really to change the fabric of reality? How can we conceive of the power of "real" magic?

Genuine Magic?

In fantasy fiction and stage magic the audience entertains the notion of human practices that produce wonders. Let's now consider purportedly genuine magic, as practiced around the world. These are ritual practices, often with an opaque causal structure, where the practitioner aims to influence or alter some outcome in the real world. As an example, in Brazil *simpátias* are forms of (often sympathetic) magic that work with animal and vegetable materials, and common household items, such as candles and coconuts. Purportedly, simpátias cure ailments (such as colds or asthma), protect infants from harm, improve interpersonal relationships (making someone fall in love with you or countering a partner's infidelity), and alleviate psychological conditions such as anxiety and depression.[24] The teeth of the caiman and the crab-eating raccoon, for instance, are used as a protection against snake bites.[25] To find a romantic partner is simple: just stick a new sharp knife into a banana tree on June 12 at midnight. Drip the liquid that leaks from the tree's wound onto a white folded piece of paper. The liquid will reveal the first letter of the name of your future partner.[26]

It is common, both in popular discourse and in ritual studies, to dismiss magical practices such as these as ineffective and therefore irrational. Indeed, the phrase "magical thinking" is synonymous with biased forms of reasoning, such as wishful thinking. A puzzle arises: if magic doesn't work, why do so many people across the world practice it? The anthropologist Bronisław Malinowski (1884–1942) attempted an answer which was based on his observations of magical practices in the Trobriand Islands (Papua New Guinea, Oceania). He noticed that people tended to rely on magic in specific contexts; namely, when the situation they were in was unpredictable and dangerous:

> While in the villages on the inner lagoon fishing is done in an easy and absolutely reliable manner by the method of poisoning, yielding abundant results without danger and uncertainty, there are on the shores of the open sea dangerous modes of fishing and also certain types in which the yield greatly varies according to whether shoals of fish appear beforehand or not. It is most significant that in the lagoon fishing, where man can rely completely on his knowledge and skill, magic does not exist, while in the open-sea fishing, full of danger and uncertainty, there is extensive magical ritual to secure safety and good results.[27]

Differently put, while people rarely use magic in situations where they have all factors under control, they might well use it to make decisions under conditions of uncertainty; doing so can have many advantages.

The anthropologist Joseph Henrich argues that apparently irrational magical practices are helpful precisely because they introduce (better) randomness than we could come up with.[28] Consider the situation in which Naskapi hunters (Cree, Canada) try to find where to hunt caribou. The hunters will have a bias to try to get to previous spots where hunting was successful. If humans were guided by past success, they would not meet the caribou, because caribou avoid such dangerous locations. For the hunters, it is better to have a randomizing device that chooses for them where to go and hunt. Naskapi hunting magic provides such a device. The hunting ritual consists of heating a caribou shoulder bone over hot coals, forming a pattern of cracks and spots. This serves as a kind of map. This pattern is essentially random, sensitive to such factors as bone density, ambient temperature, and the heat of the fire. It guides the hunters to choose a direction, which will often bring them to places where they have not killed caribou before, giving them a better chance of encountering their prey.

In a similar manner, we can explain the success of oracles for deciding whether to go to war. If you have played rock-paper-scissors, you may have noticed that humans are notably bad at randomizing their own behavior. That makes it difficult to make decisions others do not expect—for example, about the timing of an attack. Oracles such as the *yijing* (also romanized as *i ching*) and other forms of divination magic can help people to randomize better, and therefore help them to break with established patterns. In the case of a military intervention, you get the advantage of surprise this way as your move cannot be predicted by the enemy. Note that the *yijing* and hunting magic do not predict success in war and hunting. Rather, they show a path that is difficult to choose because we are so bad at randomizing; practicing them, we become successful randomizers of human behavior. This explains the success of these and other practices, such as astrology, which still has a great influence in Indian marriage practices and many other spheres of life.

We cannot explain all magical practices as instrumentally rational in this way. Nevertheless, even in instances where magical practices are ineffective or subpar, contemporary anthropologists and psychologists argue that magic is not irrational, but that it follows deep structures of human reasoning that are also deployed in science, such as causal thinking.[29] For example, magical rituals are causally opaque—we don't know exactly *how* a spell or love potion is supposed to work—but then, the same is true of the way in which laypeople use science and technology. We use GPS, vaccinations, weather reports, and computer memory, without understanding how the science behind them works. In any case, our tolerance for opacity in how things work is not irrational given how complex human technology is.

As noted at the beginning of this chapter, magic has the dual aspect of active power and passive wonder. Magical practices aim to help the practitioner gain power over her environment. This leads to an intriguing comparison with science: isn't science, like magic, a way for us to control our environment?

From Magic to Science

This similarity between magic and science did not elude early anthropologists, who discerned a deep connection between magic, religion, and science. For example, James Frazer's *Golden Bough* (1922) is a voluminous and wide-ranging tome that sketches the evolution of these practices.[30] As was common at the time, Frazer believed that all human societies move through similar stages, going from societies based on magic, to religion, to science. This staged model was abandoned in later anthropological theorizing. For one thing, if Frazer's staged model were valid, we would not expect societies that have moved on from magic to religion still to retain magical practices. However, these categories are fluid and often occur within a single society. Contemporary US cultures, for example, rely heavily on science, but there is also a continued importance of religion in both the public and the private sphere, and magic is practiced in a wide range of settings, from Instawitches to traditional procedures to ward off the evil eye.

Though Frazer thought magic was an earlier (and less developed) stage compared to religion or science, he didn't think belief in magic was necessarily irrational. Indeed, he drew attention to structural similarities between modern science and magic:

> Underlying the whole system is a faith, implicit but real and firm, in the order and uniformity of nature. The magician does not doubt that the same causes will always produce the same effects, that the performance of the proper ceremony, accompanied by the appropriate spell, will inevitably be attended by the desired result.[31]

The magician doesn't seek the supernatural intervention of a god, but rather, like a scientist, "he strictly conforms to the rules of his art or to what may be called the laws of nature as conceived by him."[32] Magic and science share commonalities, such as the desire of magicians/scientists to directly intervene, by using empirically observable regularities, in a replicable manner.

The anthropologist Marcel Mauss criticized Frazer's cultural evolutionism.[33] However, he agreed with Frazer that magic is linked to science, as well as technology: "It is not only a practical art, it is also a storehouse of ideas. It attaches great importance to knowledge [. . . ;] as far as magic is concerned, knowledge is power."[34] In Mauss's view, magic is practical, less concerned with metaphysics than religion is, and more preoccupied with understanding nature. Mauss believed magic lies at the basis of the sciences in what he called primitive societies (roughly, this meant Indigenous and pre-literate societies) and in ancient Greece. He saw in the magical practices of such societies the beginnings of astronomy, medicine, natural history, and the physical sciences.

We see a similar genealogy from magic to science in the work of philosopher and social scientist Otto Neurath (1882–1945), which ties into his politically progressive ideas. Neurath was one of the co-founders of the Vienna Circle (Wiener Kreis) in 1924, together with philosopher Moritz Schlick and mathematician Hans Hahn. The members of the Vienna Circle met on Thursday evenings to discuss fundamental questions in the philosophy of science. They pondered the nature of science, what made statements meaningful, and how logic could be used to improve lucidity. They were committed to clarity of thought, against obscurantism and theological and metaphysical baggage. This was practically relevant, as Austria (along with other German-speaking countries) was mired in growing populism, Nazism, and antisemitism. Clarity of thought could counter emotion-based propaganda and political dogma, or so the Vienna Circle members hoped. In their 1929 manifesto, they insist that "the scientific world-conception knows no *unsolvable riddle*."[35] This picture of science was connected to a broader concern with collective human life, notably public education and social reform. For the members of the Vienna Circle,

> [t]he representatives of this scientific-world conception resolutely stand on the ground of simple human experience. They confidently approach the task of removing the metaphysical and theological debris of millennia. Or, as some have it: returning, after a metaphysical interlude, to a unified picture of this world which had, in a sense, been at the basis of magical beliefs, free from theology, in the earliest times.[36]

Otto Neurath developed this idea of science as an heir to magic further in his 1931 paper "Empirical Sociology." Magic is the ancestor of a unified science, such as that which he and others were hoping to develop. Or, differently put, magic is rooted in the same commonsensical, practical thinking that also motivates science. He denied that magic was a special mode of thinking that one would only find in Indigenous societies. Rather, "pre-animistic magic, probably the oldest, is akin to our behavior. But animistic magic too is like modern behavior, directed toward finite, earthly ends."[37] Magic, like science, is concerned with practical purposes and empirical observation, and is unlike theology, which is laden with metaphysics and obscure thought. Hence, "[m]agic does not mean something mysterious, *only the poor, hardwon techniques of social existence of primitive peoples.*"[38]

Neurath spearheaded efforts to improve the housing of working-class people and to provide them with adult education, as well as disseminating picture-based statistical information to them (akin to infographics now). He saw working-class people as resembling Indigenous people, concerned with the practicalities of life, and striving to solve concrete problems that their natural and social environments pose. Magicians, like scientists, try to find causal connections in opaque phenomena:

> What we have of systematic and orderly action and speech thus seems to go back to primeval systematic orderliness as found in magic. The scientific tendency to link everything with everything else, to regard nothing as indifferent, clearly already belonged to the age of magic.[39]

In that respect, science is a return to the practicality of magic. It discards religious dogma and metaphysics and focuses on repeatable, stable features of our environment. Unlike what its reputation suggests, science is not obscure or elitist—because of its practicality, it is the opposite.

This genealogical picture has problems. For one thing, it implicitly draws upon cultural evolutionism, which is an incorrect historical framework. However, there are more recent attempts to derive science from magic, that look at the evolution of early modern science.

The Magical Roots of Early Modern Science

Current research on the origins of science and its connection to magic could not have happened without the influential work by Frances Yates (1899–1981), a historian of Renaissance science. She was largely self-taught (with a BA in French, and no degree in history) and wrote with literary flair and an adventurous hermeneutical scope, compelling later generations of historians to consider the role of magic in Renaissance philosophy and culture, which is now standardly acknowledged.[40]

In her seminal *Giordano Bruno and the Hermetic Tradition* (1964), Yates took another look at why the Italian philosopher Giordano Bruno (1548–1600) was tried for heresy. In her account, Bruno wasn't burned at the stake because of his scientific ideas, but because of his work in hermeticism. He worked as a Renaissance magus: that is, a philosopher who aimed to gain knowledge through secret means, drawing on the Kabbalah (Jewish mystical texts), and the Hermetica (purportedly, ancient texts written by a legendary figure, Hermes Trismegistus). The central focus on wonder in hermetic magic led Bruno to accept heliocentrism. In doing so, he wasn't motivated so much by calculations or astronomical evidence, but by, amongst other things, his sense of wonder at the infinite cosmos, "those magnificent stars and luminous bodies which are so many inhabited worlds, great creatures and superlative divinities: those which seem to be, and are, innumerable worlds not very unlike that in which we find ourselves."[41]

Other hermetic authors include Giovanni Pico della Mirandola (Italy), Heinrich Cornelius Agrippa (Germany), and John

Dee (England). In Yates's account, magic and science are separate endeavors, though there are connections and flows between them, as in Bruno's acceptance of a scientific theory (heliocentrism) for occult and magical reasons.[42] Her work drew attention to magical and mystical elements in the scientific revolution which had been airbrushed out of the history of science. The term "Yates thesis" became shorthand for a stronger claim, that she didn't make: the claim that the early modern scientific revolution evolved directly out of Renaissance magic, occultism, and hermeticism.[43]

Nevertheless, contemporary historians of science who specialize in the philosophy of magic recognize the enduring influence of Yates's work. Some elements of her theory are still attractive: science is indebted to some extent to magic, notably in the openness of Renaissance magicians to doing experiments as a way to gain knowledge. As Mark Waddell argues, throughout antiquity and the medieval period, natural philosophers thought the best way to figure out how nature works is simply to observe it under its usual (i.e., natural) conditions, using one's natural faculties, without aids such as telescopes or microscopes.[44] In this Aristotelian picture, doing experiments makes no sense, as an experimental situation does not spontaneously occur under natural conditions. To *manipulate* nature, as early proponents of the experimental method such as Francis Bacon (1561–1626) proposed, was an innovation. The hands-on character of this new paradigm could be found in many early precursors of science, such as alchemy and hermetic magic. Recent work in the history and philosophy of science, moreover, shows that early magic was much more empirically sophisticated than previously believed; see, for example, the enduring influence of magic and alchemy in the work of early scientists such as the chemistry of Robert Boyle.[45]

We can see a demonstration of this connection between magic and early modern science in Bruno's treatise on magic, which starts out with a series of definitions of "magician" and "magic." In line with other writers of the early modern period, Bruno connects magic to wonder:

> "Magician" refers to someone who does wondrous things merely by manipulating active and passive powers, as occurs in chemistry, medicine and such fields; this is commonly called "natural magic."[46]

Here, Bruno refers to the tendency of magicians, unlike natural philosophers, to directly manipulate the natural materials and observe the effects of these manipulations.

Now, we would call these magicians "scientists." However, the term "scientist" was only coined in the nineteenth century, by William Whewell in a review of Mary Somerville's *On the Connexion of the Physical Sciences* (1834),[47] which sought to popularize results from the sciences.[48] Whewell chose the term "scientist" for lack of a better alternative—he considered, among others, "savans" (too French), "philosopher" (too lofty), and "nature-poker" or even "nature-peeper," but considered neither of these alternatives palatable. It is interesting then, that Bruno uses the word "magician" to refer to people who manipulate nature. He continues with an account of natural magic:

> Magic refers to what happens as a result of the powers of attraction and repulsion between things, for example, the pushes, motions and attractions due to magnets and such things, when all these actions are due not to active and passive qualities but rather to the spirit or soul existing in things. This is called "natural magic" in the proper sense.[49]

Magnets, the tides, and other anomalous phenomena that did not obey the way things normally behave (at least, according to Bruno's contemporaries) were classified under natural magic and became the objects of study of Renaissance magi. Theirs was the study of the wonders of nature. A mere two centuries later, science had taken the place of natural magic, and magic came to acquire the pejorative connotation it still has today. But rather than saying (as we might conventionally do) that science disenchanted the world, we might say rather that science became enchanted by magical practices.[50]

In this chapter, I have argued that the cognitive basis for magic and magical practice is wonder, combined with a desire for control. Magic encompasses the human practices that harness a perceived, intended, or feigned ability to produce wonders. Through magic, we work wonders. Science, as we will see in chapter 6, is also wondrous.

5

Seeing with Firstness

RELIGION AS AWE- AND WONDER-TECHNOLOGY

The Anthropologist's Secret

"I felt like I was going to be possessed. Of course, I knew it wasn't possible, there's no such thing as spirits. Still, in the heat of the moment, I feared I would be their next victim," the anthropologist said, fingers clenched around her large beer mug as she relived the experience. The year was 2009, the place a riverside pub close to the Oxford college of Christ Church. I was enrolled in an intensive summer workshop for scholars in the humanities to learn quantitative methods in the study of religion, to be specific, the cognitive science of religion. We were a diverse bunch: philosophers, anthropologists, historians, and religious studies scholars. Hands down, the anthropologists had the most exciting stories to tell. They traveled to far-flung places, studying the religious beliefs of Mongolian shamans, Indigenous Peruvians, and Balinese Hindus. Many of them shared a secret—they had experiences they believed were impossible.

The anthropologist I spoke to had done fieldwork on spirit possession in Brazil. A committed atheist and materialist, she never once believed the spirits were real. Rather, she was interested in the cultural and cognitive factors that lead people to believe in spirit possession. Yet, during a ceremony in the Amazon rainforest, where she saw one person after another falling into the thrall of possession, she could not shake off the fear that she too might become possessed. The other anthropologists in our little group agreed: once you study a set of religious beliefs for long enough, and you're able to participate in the rituals, you start *seeing things*. Such "anomalous experiences" are common among anthropologists immersed in fieldwork.[1] They will experience events that are difficult to explain in naturalistic terms. James McClenon and Jennifer Nooney have documented and analyzed forty such cases in the published literature. Anthropologists tend to not accept these experiences as real: once they're back in their familiar surroundings, they shrug them off as side effects of tiredness, stress, or getting too carried away.

Anomalous experiences serve as a useful reminder of the power of religious ideas and practices. Because religious beliefs and practices are so ubiquitous—and have been domesticated, as it were, in the form of syrupy messages on pre-printed greetings cards—we tend to forget they profoundly shape how we experience the world. Religions drive people to amazing deeds of self-sacrifice or love, but they also lead to terrible things, such as ecological destruction, human sacrifice, and warfare. To anthropologists and other scholars who study religion, its power to shape how we think and act has been a long-term puzzle. In a naturalistic framework, there's no room for spirits, gods, and other religious entities. Why, then, do people devote to religion so much time, effort, and material resources which could (it seems) have been more profitably spent on so many other causes?

The Cognitive Science of Religion

We can approach the question of religion through the cognitive science of religion (CSR), the multidisciplinary cognitive study of religious beliefs and practices. Authors in this field hold that the diversity of religious beliefs and practices, great though it is, is constrained by the structure of the human mind. CSR authors take inspiration from the *epidemiology of representations*, a theoretical framework devised by the French anthropologist Dan Sperber.[2] This framework makes an analogy between the transmission of culture and the transmission of infectious diseases. To understand how infectious diseases transmit, we need to know not only about viruses, bacteria, and other pathogens, but also about the human body and how it interacts with its environment. Imagine if you wanted to understand how HIV transmits, and you only looked at the structure of the virus. This would give a woefully incomplete picture of HIV, because the virus needs human hosts and relies on propensities of the human body and behavior to be transmitted from one host to another.

Similarly, Sperber holds, if we only study cultural elements in the scientific study of culture, we end up with an incomplete picture. Ideas don't jump from one mind to another. They require a process whereby ideas are made publicly available by one person, in language or in some item of material culture (e.g., a drawing or sculpture), and are reconstructed in the minds of the people attending to this one person or material object. Thus, understanding culture requires that we gain insight into the structure of the human mind. This way of thinking marks a departure from an earlier consensus in the study of religion, which held that culture shapes our minds, not the other way around. CSR authors acknowledge the influence of culture on our behavior and perceptions, but they argue that our minds also limit what sorts of religious beliefs and practices get transmitted.

CSR doesn't have an overarching concept of what religion might be, and doesn't try to define it. As cognitive scientist Claire White points out, this puzzles people from outside the field.[3] In order to study religion, shouldn't you get clear on what "religion" means? CSR authors prefer to discuss the constituent parts of religion, such as theological beliefs, ritual practices, or myths, rather than religion as a whole. "Religion" as a shorthand covers a wide range of phenomena that we commonly call religion. While there might be borderline cases (e.g., is astrology religion? Or is it just part of some religious systems?), there are many instances of human behavior and belief that we do accept as religious: for example, belief in gods, origin myths, and rituals. CSR investigates the origins, cultural spread, and persistence of such elements. Following the lead of other CSR authors, I will not attempt to define religion, but rather use the term to mean what we commonly tend to denote as "religion." This is a comparative concept, which gradually and organically grew over the past centuries and which typically encompasses beliefs, rituals, and dietary and vestimentary practices.[4]

The views of CSR authors span a wide range, but they agree that there is an intimate connection between cognition and culture: our minds shape religious beliefs and practices, and those, in turn, shape us. However, there is disagreement about what the nature of that relationship is. One influential position holds that religious beliefs are simply a by-product of how the mind works. Pascal Boyer and Bob McCauley are proponents of this view.[5] They argue that there is something about religious beliefs that make them uniquely memorable and easy to transmit.

Take the concept of *revenant* in Europe or *gwisin* in Korean folklore. Both concepts are about a (usually recently) deceased person who haunts the living in some embodied form due to unfinished business. What makes belief in this widespread? The answer lies in the way we think about other people, their psychology, and their motivations. We spontaneously attribute beliefs and desires to people, even when they are out of sight and out of contact (for instance, because they moved abroad and you've lost touch). A person's death doesn't hamper our ability to think about what they might feel or do. One of the postdocs and co-organizers of the Oxford workshop mentioned above had suddenly died shortly before the event. As one of the other organizers said, "I still sometimes see him in the hallways. I know it's not possible of course, but it's hard to shake the feeling of his presence." When a cultural idea pops up that incorporates such beliefs, it becomes memorable and has a higher chance of being transmitted. The idea of a *revenant* or *gwisin* isn't particularly useful to us. It might even be harmful, causing unnecessary fear and distress. However, the structure of our psychology explains why our minds are vulnerable to the idea of returning dead. They are, then, just a by-product of how the mind works.

The by-product view is influential in CSR, but an alternative approach is rapidly gaining ground. According to this view, religion is adaptive. It helps us survive and reproduce. Defenders of this position include anthropologists Ben Purzycki and Rich Sosis who argue that religion is biologically adaptive.[6] It is analogous to a spider's web, or a beaver's dam. It is not a part of our body, but it still helps us to solve adaptive problems that humans recurrently face. Sosis has spent many years researching religion in Israeli communities, and he found, for example, that religious kibbutzim (voluntary cooperative communities that are traditionally based on agricultural labor) are more profitable and survive for longer periods than secular kibbutzim, and that their kibbutznikim cooperate better.

In the nineteenth century the US witnessed a proliferation of communes in which early European settlers experimented with very different, often utopian ways of living and being. These could include, for example, discouragement of marriage and lack of private property. Some of these communes were founded on the basis of religious ideas; others were secular. Sosis and Eric Bressler found that the secular experiments were much more short-lived than the religious ones: in any given year, a secular commune was three times more likely to dissolve than a religious one.[7] In Sosis's view, religion helps groups achieve better cooperation by establishing hard-to-fake signals, such as customs of dress, practices of alcohol abstinence, sexual practices, and customs of music. You would not abide by these norms unless you were a committed member of the religious group.

While I think the by-product view has a lot of explanatory potential, the accumulation of evidence in favor of some adaptive functions of religion has become significant.[8] This does not mean that every religious practice is adaptive, or that religions have better solutions to adaptive problems compared to secular alternatives. In my view, religion is a set of cognitive technologies that we employ to serve enduring human needs.[9] We don't only engage in religious practices because we fall prey to cognitive biases, as in the *revenant* or *gwisin* example. Religion helps us to engage with our environment. Just as we use electronic calculators, abacuses, counting rods, and long division to help us solve mathematical problems, religion can help us solve existential problems. Religion comforts and consoles us, makes us feel on top of things when the world spins out of control, and in general helps us to deal with the many curveballs life throws at us. This harks back to anthropologist Leslie White's remarks (discussed in chapter 1) that religion fulfills human needs, particularly needs that are not material, but existential and emotional.

Philosopher Stephen Asma argues that religion helps us to manage our emotional lives, and in this way, our relationships with each other.[10] Take terror management theory, which says that the success of religion is in part due to its ability to make us believe we might survive our physical death. The realization that we, or people we care about, will die one day is a scary—sometimes even debilitating—thought. Religions with a (preferably attractive) view of the afterlife soften that blow and make life in the present moment more enjoyable. Asma thinks religion solves emotion-management problems more consistently than do secular alternatives.

While religion is very effective at emotion-management, and I will focus on this particular aspect of it, it does more than this. For example, it helps regulate marriage systems: many religions, such as Christianity and Islam, place limits on the number of women one can be married to simultaneously (respectively, one and four). This prevents the formation of groups of single men who cannot marry because the marriage market is monopolized by a few wealthy individuals, and staves off resentment and violence as a result. Religions also regulate interactions with our environment, often (but unfortunately not always) with an eye toward increased sustainability.[11] For example, the Bali water temple system helps farmers coordinate and fairly divide water for irrigation. Moreover, its festivals and ceremonies time the planting and harvesting of rice. Thanks to this religious system, Balinese farmers can subsist sustainably on rice, with high population densities. Moreover, as I will show, religion also makes accessible to us emotional registers that would otherwise not be available. Such emotional registers are sometimes key to helping us address various human needs. A sense of wonder can pull us out of unhelpful ruts or can save us from despair and drudgery. Religion can help us to rekindle this emotional register.

Maurice Merleau-Ponty on Religious Habits

The idea that religion helps us modulate our emotions is ancient. The Chinese philosopher Xunzi argued that our mental lives are a disorganized mess, and that our emotions cause social friction.[12] Fortunately, we have cultural means (or, as he terms it, "artifice" or *wei*) to fix ourselves. Xunzi lived during the Warring States period (ca. 475–221 BCE), a war-torn, eventful time in Chinese history. Before China was unified in a single empire, it consisted of a patchwork of states. Large states invaded smaller ones, taxes skyrocketed, and forced conscription of young men into the army was rife. On top of this, people suffered frequent devastating plagues and famines. Xunzi argued that religious ceremonies and music help us to live together harmoniously, because they nurture our desires. He begins his “Discourse on Ritual”—the ninth chapter of his eponymous book *Xunzi*—with the simple question, “From what did ritual arise?” He locates the answer to this question in human desires. We have desires and needs that don’t have a clear limit. If not properly checked, we will struggle (in warfare, thievery, unhealthy competition) and end up impoverished. However, ritual responds to our needs in a way that doesn’t deplete material resources—that is sustainable. Just as cooked food nurtures our palates, perfume nurtures our noses, and music nurtures our ears, ritual, in Xunzi’s view, nurtures the mind, taking care of our emotional and cognitive needs.

One of those needs is a need for awe and wonder. As I’ll show, awe and wonder not only make us feel good; they also challenge our thinking. If we accept the idea that religion nurtures our response to enduring human needs and desires, we can take a closer look at its role in fostering awe and wonder. I propose that some religious practices are *awe-technologies*. They help us to kindle a sense of awe and wonder, at both our natural and our social environment. These awe-technologies transform how we see the world: due to a sustained sense of awe and wonder, we engage with the world (and with other creatures) in an altered way.

Habits play a crucial role in our engagement with the world. Phenomenologists such as Martin Heidegger (1889–1976) and Maurice Merleau-Ponty (1908–1961) recognized this. One way we perceive the world is as a collection of *affordances*: things in our environment that invite us to engage with it in a certain way.[13] This way of perceiving the world shapes both our small and our big decisions, and how we generally go about in our lives. Take Chiara, a neuroscience major who plays the cello in her spare time. When in her flat, she sees her instrument (prominent and large) sitting in the corner of a room as “for-playing.” When she opens her fridge, she spies a piece of leftover pizza as "for-eating." These affordances don't all present themselves as equally salient. A sense of hunger makes the pizza more prominent in her mind, cueing her that it is for-eating. Maybe Chiara is worried about upcoming exams, and doesn't think she can make the time to play her instrument. That makes it less for-playing than when she has plenty of time and just listened to a moving cello concerto.

Engaging with our environment doesn't require that we make conscious decisions all the time (about whether to eat the slice of pizza or play the cello); rather, we often rely on habits. Merleau-Ponty argued that habits help us to respond to the world without having to think consciously about our decisions. Over time, we cultivate habits through practice, and in due course, they become automatic. Chiara sees her cello catch the warm afternoon sun. She picks it up, almost unthinkingly, and plays as a warm-up exercise Bach's prelude from the Cello Suite no. 1 in G Major (BVW 1007), a piece she knows by heart (as many cellists do). She doesn't need to consciously will herself to do this. In fact, willing yourself to do things all the time quickly leads to a sense of exhaustion and decision fatigue. Habits such as Chiara's shape our general responses to the world, from the moment we step out of bed to when we go to sleep.

Merleau-Ponty sees habits as embodied things we do, such as when we play a musical instrument, or drive to the supermarket. They are not purely automatic, like a knee-jerk reflex, but we don't control them intellectually either. Rather, the fluency of our habits is a result of hard-won expertise. In this way, habits are like skills. Our skillful habits aren't separate from the rest of our lived experience. They are an integral part of it, particularly of our projects. These are activities we set out to do with a specific goal. Our habits "polarize the world, bringing magically to view a host of signs which guide action, as notices in a museum guide the visitor."[14] This is why acquiring a habit takes effort, but once you master it, it allows you to offload a lot of decision-making. Your everyday environment where your habits are situated will help you make these decisions. As Komarine Romdenh-Romluc summarizes it, "When one develops a habit, one both acquires a pattern of behavior and a way of perceiving the world—one comes to perceive relevant parts of the world as offering opportunities to perform the habitual actions."[15]

Religions are powerful habit-shapers. They shift our affordances, just like the notices in a museum. Take Jim, who converted to Islam. Before his conversion, as a lukewarm Christian and a non-vegetarian, he would see bacon as for-eating. He enjoyed his regular slice of bacon for breakfast, or as a snack. He can no longer eat bacon since becoming an observant Muslim, because Islam has a prohibition on eating pork. Jim also needs to pray five times a day, arranging his busy schedule as a lawyer to accommodate this. During Ramadan, he's unable to eat or drink anything from sunrise to sunset. This is hard, especially when Ramadan falls in a period with many daylight hours. Yet, being a lawyer, Jim needs to accommodate this strict religious practice along with his demanding day job. His non-Muslim friends and relatives see Islam as limiting: Jim has to give up bacon! How tough that Ramadan falls in July this year! They see his religious practices as foreclosing possibilities he used to have in his life. But for Jim, being a Muslim is not about prohibitions, but about acquiring new habits. He has come to embrace fasting; he is not tempted by bacon, because his newly acquired dietary habits (of eating halal) make bacon not-for-eating.

The idea of religion as something that limits its adherents is a partial picture. For one thing, choosing to be bound by your habits constitutes also a kind of freedom—a position Erik Rietveld has explored in detail.[16] Without habits, each individual decision becomes a cognitive load which may lead to decision-fatigue. Religion can help to alleviate this by precluding a number of options. At the same time, religion opens up a world of possibilities, a world that is only available to you because you habituate yourself into its beliefs and practices. Take Samuel, who was born in a secular Jewish household. As he grew up, he decided to deepen his commitment to Judaism. He began to live in line with orthodox Jewish requirements, such as strictly observing the sabbath and not mixing meat and cheese. Sam is now an academic, and like all academics, finds it hard to achieve good work–life balance. Early-career academics have to sacrifice their weekends, or so Sam believes. However, as an observant Jew he cannot work from Friday to Saturday evening. Much like Merleau-Ponty's museum notices guiding the visitor, religious habits guide his life, and offer him new ways to engage with and respond to what happens in it. Not being able to work one day a week affords Samuel a sense of freedom that many academics envy.

Anthropologist Tanya Luhrmann has provided a detailed case study of how religious habits can shape our perception of reality. This focuses on Vineyard Charismatic Evangelical Christians, who incorporate their personal relationship with God into their everyday, mundane experiences. In order to experience God, they have to acquire a new theory of mind, one whereby some thoughts that seem to originate within their own mind are attributed to God. They conceptualize their mind as a porous entity, where God's thoughts permeate their own thinking. To understand how these Christians learn to experience God in this way, Luhrmann joined two Vineyard communities, one in Chicago and one in Palo Alto (two cities where she was living and teaching), for a duration of four years.

> One of the first things a person must master at a church like the Vineyard is to recognize when God is present and when he responds [. . .]. Newcomers soon learn that God is understood to speak to congregants inside their own minds. They learn that someone who worships God at the Vineyard must develop the ability to recognize thoughts in their mind that are in fact not their thoughts, but God's. They learn that this is a skill they must master.[17]

Luhrmann suggests that ordinary sense perception (such as hearing or seeing God) is a poor analogy for mystical perception. In many cases, mystical perception is more akin to a specialized skill, analogous to the skilled perceptions of scientists and art connoisseurs. In order to acquire this skillset, practitioners need to develop various habits. These include reading scripture, prayer (both solitary and with others), and communal worship. Some of these practices involve deliberate pretense as a way to heighten one's experience of God. For example, a pastor encouraged members of his congregation to make coffee for two, pouring an extra cup for God. Some female congregants went on a date night with God.[18] These practices help Vineyard community members to experience God in their everyday lives. In what follows, I will look at how religious practices can make us more receptive to awe and wonder, and more likely to experience them.

Religious Practice, Awe, and Wonder

Maurice Merleau-Ponty was not religious. A lapsed Roman Catholic, he abandoned the Church over its political positions, and what he felt was an inherent ambiguity. Contrasting the revolutionary spirit of Jesus's core teachings with the conservatism of the religion he grew up in, Merleau-Ponty wrote that Catholicism "can be revolutionary, but the religion of the Father is conservative."[19] Following the Austrian government's shelling of working-class districts in Vienna in 1934 and the Church's lackluster response to this, he commented that a Christian is "a poor conservative and an unsafe bet as a revolutionary."[20] A Christian's loyalties are split, and part of them will always go to an inherently conservative institution, the Catholic Church, which is "a machine, an institution or a movement" that goes in a "reactionary direction."[21]

Yet, at the same time Merleau-Ponty was fascinated by the religious impulse of people across times and cultures. What draws us so irresistibly to religion? To answer that question, we need to look at the broader picture of wonder in Merleau-Ponty's work. In the "Preface" to his *Phenomenology of Perception* (1945), he asks what phenomenology is. His enigmatic answer (that he clarifies later on) is that phenomenology is a philosophy that puts essences back into existence. He faults Descartes and Kant for detaching the subject from experience and making the grasping of the self (captured in Descartes's *cogito* argument, "I think, therefore I am") as primary: as a precondition before you can know anything about the world.[22]

In Merleau-Ponty's interpretation, phenomenology is the rejection of the primacy of the self over and above our environment. We are so enmeshed with the world that the only way to notice what is going on in it, and in ourselves, is to suspend and "put out of play" our engagements with the world: "because in order to arouse them and bring them to view, we have to suspend for a moment our recognition of them."[23] This is what philosophy does. Philosophy is "'wonder' in the face of the world."[24] But wonder doesn't mean withdrawing from the world. Rather, philosophy "steps back to watch the forms of transcendence fly up like sparks from a fire; it slackens the intentional threads which attach us to the world and thus brings them to our notice."[25] Phenomenology draws on, and is nurtured by, this sense of wonder. Because we are limited creatures who exist as part of the world, the world will necessarily strike us as mysterious. Religious beliefs and practices are ways to engage with this continued sense of mystery.

Merleau-Ponty's views on skill and habit offer us a new way to think about religion. As philosopher Jack Williams points out, an important development in the philosophy of religion has been a recent move away from a belief-centric view of religion.[26] After all, religion is not just a set of beliefs; it is also—and in some cases, is first and foremost—a set of practices, including liturgy, prayer, fasting, and festivals.[27]

Phenomenology by itself is not sufficient to help us make a shift toward increased attention for the philosophical significance of such practices. But Merleau-Ponty's focus on habits is crucial, as he explains how religious habits can be part of one's lived experience, and shape how we view the world. By training oneself in specific habits,

> [a] human being may freely choose to exploit the physical, affective, and habitual capacities of her body to pursue projects that would otherwise be closed off. This is the technique adopted by, for example, a virtuoso pianist, for whom habit and practice are essential in opening up new projects and possibilities. It is also the approach taken by a religious practitioner—a Christian monk in the mystical tradition, for example—to open up spiritual projects and possibilities denied to the uninitiated novice.[28]

Good Wonder, Bad Wonder

Let's see how religion can be a cognitive technology that helps us to harness a sense of awe and wonder. Through the practice of religious habits, we open up new possibilities to experience awe and wonder at things that we've long grown used to. Religious practices can be apt to help us keep bad awe and wonder at bay, while also cultivating awe and wonder that are useful and regulative for us. Let us briefly recapitulate Descartes's idea that wonder (his concept of *admiration*, which encompasses both awe and wonder) is the passion of firstness. Recall that in his view, "wonder is a sudden surprise of the soul which brings it to consider with attention the objects that seem to it unusual and extraordinary."[29] It is the first of the passions that occurs before we begin to evaluate something positively or negatively. Rather than imposing our existing conceptual schemas onto whatever causes wonder in us, we allow it to challenge us and to reconsider them.

However, while Descartes accepts that wonder is useful, he also fears it can go awry. Unchecked wonder can lead us down unhealthy and obscure rabbit holes. Consider Mira, a homemaker who browses the internet and chances upon videos that propagate the false idea that the earth is flat. The videos persuade her that the earth is not round, and the evidence she thought she had (e.g., pictures of the earth from space) is false. Her wonder about this encourages her to rethink her schemas about Earth being a round planet, and this brings about an even greater sense of wonder. This brief example indicates that under some conditions unchecked wonder can indeed be harmful, fueling conspiracy thinking. It is unchecked because it is unwarranted: there is no compelling reason for Mira to rethink her earlier belief that the earth is round. Therefore, Descartes thought that, once wonder had helped us achieve knowledge, we should rid ourselves of it as soon as possible, because then we can think straight again.

Here, I want to maintain the Cartesian idea that unchecked wonder can be harmful, but I think (contra Descartes) that wonder remains useful even after we have acquired knowledge. We are just a tiny part of a big universe, and there will always be aspects of it that elude our understanding. No scientific (or other) beliefs will be definite or above challenge, and hence we will always need wonder to challenge the preconceived ideas we have.[30] Because familiarity makes us lose our sense of wonder, we need to resensitize ourselves to the world, *pace* Descartes. I explore the following idea: some religious beliefs and practices constitute a cognitive technology that helps us regulate our sense of awe and wonder by enabling us to see with firstness. To this end, I draw on Heschel's discussion of awe and wonder in his philosophy of Judaism.

Abraham Joshua Heschel (1907–1972) was a Polish-born rabbi and scholar of Jewish thought. He moved to the UK to escape the Nazis, who killed his three sisters and his mother. Later he migrated to the US, where he took up a position at the Jewish Theological Seminary of America in New York City, where he lectured until his death. His works are focused on Judaism and have a broad appeal, particularly *Man is Not Alone* (1951) and *God in Search of Man* (1955). These books articulate a philosophy of Judaism which highlights the significance of both Jewish thought and Jewish practice for a contemporary audience. In Heschel's view, "[r]eligion is an answer to man's central questions."[31] The main task of the philosophy of religion is to rediscover what questions religion is an answer to. Heschel means by these questions more than just questions about the origin of humans, or the universe. They also include existential questions, such as what our lives mean, and how we should live them.

The challenge that Heschel saw, both for religion and for philosophical reflection on it, is that people take the world for granted. Because we have become complacent, and primarily trust in science and technology to solve our problems, we have lost the ability to experience nature with depth and reverence. We rely on solutions that science offers without pausing to think about the marvels that science has revealed to us. Techno-optimism is a recent symptom of this complacency, as we can see in the vague gesturing toward, for example, carbon capture to reverse global warming. This conceit is misplaced because it makes us think we can go on polluting and over-extracting natural resources without a need for re-evaluation. We simply trust that science and technology will defeat any problems that arise. However, Heschel believed this was a dangerous idea. Awe and wonder are the antidotes to this misplaced smugness.

Heschel held that emotions are a kind of cognitive technology—things we engage in purposively to change the world.[32] They can help us to see the world not in flat, drab, and purely instrumental terms, but as filled with marvels, valuable for its own sake. Deep knowledge, of the kind attained by profound scientific insight or, for Heschel, religious wisdom, requires that we see the world as an end, beautiful in itself. And to achieve that, awe is required.

Heschel argued that Jewish rituals are conducive to awe. For example, orthodox Jews utter blessings at particular occasions: when they see a rainbow, when they notice the first fragile blossoms on fruit trees, when they meet a wise person, or hear good news. These blessings are embodied physical actions that one performs to mark certain emotional states in response to the environment. The repetition of such ritual practices trains our minds and bodies to respond with awe and wonder to the world around us. By uttering a blessing, you become more attuned to how precious and fleeting these things are. For Heschel, rituals are not a form of adjusting yourself to the world. They are the opposite; they are about maladjustment. "Wonder or radical amazement, the state of maladjustment to words and notions, is therefore a prerequisite for an authentic awareness of that which is."[33] The blessings thus afford a kind of mystical experience, writ small.[34]

Conceived this way, Jewish rituals help us out of our dulled complacency, and allow us to see the world in a new light. They are not some simple kind of mind-hack. Rather, they are deeply transformative, beckoning us to experience the world (again) in an authentic way. But Heschel also cautions against badly directed awe and wonder, such as at political leaders, money, or material objects, or at nature itself—which, though it can evoke awe and wonder is not, in Heschel's view, worthy of worship. None of these things is "worthy of our supreme adoration, love, sacrifice, or self-dedication."[35] Religion is rooted in both awe and wonder. It is a starting point of what we do with these emotions; it is "not a feeling for the mystery of living, or a sense of awe, wonder and fear, which is the root of religion, but rather the question *of what to do* with the feeling for the mystery of the living, what to do with awe, wonder, or fear."[36] Heschel's idea of skilled seeing through religious practice accords well with Merleau-Ponty's ideas on skill and habit, as we will explore in the next section.

Religion and the Skill of Seeing with Firstness

The idea that religious belief-formation draws on skillful practices was explored by William Alston.[37] He discussed the role of doxastic practices (practices that help us to form certain beliefs) in mystical perception. While doxastic practices are, for him, generic high-level processes such as visual perception, we can see that more deliberate and religion-specific practices are crucial to mystical experience. The latter form an integral part of the contemplative life, as is clear in the writings of the Catholic nun Teresa of Ávila (1515–1582) and the Sufi master Ibn Tufayl (ca. 1110–1185). Both mystics describe perceiving God as a gradual journey of spiritual discovery that requires discipline and training. Teresa likens the soul of the believer to a castle with layers of inner courts that one can enter through spiritual training.[38] Ibn Tufayl tells the parable of a young boy living on a desert island, brought up by gazelles, who discovers all by himself halal dietary restrictions, long periods of contemplation (*tafakur*), and Sufi physical exercises, and thus comes to experience God.[39]

Contemplative practices like these are all too often discarded as a waste of time. At best, they're reduced to mind-hacks or productivity enhancers, divorced from their spiritual and metaphysical roots, as in the case of Zen meditation or Stoic spiritual exercises as touted by wellness gurus. It would be an impoverishment, though, to reduce contemplative practices to mere means to fulfill our role in producing work or capital. Rather, some of these religious practices aim at rediscovering our sense of firstness by making us again receptive to awe and wonder. In a sense, you habituate yourself in order to dishabituate yourself.

How can religious practices awaken a sense of wonder? As we saw earlier, our habits make some aspects of our environment jump out at us, helping us to shape our decisions, and hence our agency. We can perceive a musical instrument as for-playing if we create a habit of practicing regularly. But seeing with awe and wonder is seeing something "not-for-something." It takes the object or event as it is, meeting it on its own terms, allowing it to change us and, particularly, our frame of reference. Recall that for Descartes, awe and wonder occur when we encounter an object before we have decided how we will use it, or even whether we should be happy about it, or dislike it. Heschel suggests that religion, such as the Jewish practice of blessings, allows us to recover this sense of firstness. There are blessings for a wide range of occasions, even for receiving bad news: "Baruch dayan ha'emet" (Blessed is the True Judge) is said upon hearing exceptionally bad news, often someone's death. There are also blessings for mundane pleasures, such as when eating fruit or vegetables. These blessings help us to recover a sense of awe and wonder at getting nourishment, and open the mind beyond a simple utilitarian perspective on food. The blessings do not guarantee that we greet these events—hearing news, eating food, seeing beautiful things—with awe and wonder. But they open the mental space for us to do so; they guard against going through life as merely going through the motions.

A potential objection to the view that religious practices can serve as wonder-technology is that repetition will inevitably lead to familiarity. The first time you hear a religious miracle story you are amazed, say, at how Moses parts the Red Sea, Jesus raises a girl from the dead, or lotuses sprout wherever the infant Buddha walks. But hearing these stories time after time will lessen your sense of wonder. We thus need a clearer picture of how religious cognitive technologies can guard against this, and keep on instilling wonder.

A clue comes from the work of two cognitive scientists, Ulrich Weger and Johannes Wagemann, who used an introspective approach to investigate the phenomenology of wonder.[40] The aim of their study was to differentiate wonder from awe. Qualitative studies are useful to help map out a conceptual landscape and to find certain patterns that quantitative methods (with fewer open-ended questions) miss. The method employed by these researchers was to simply write down experiences of awe and wonder over a period of approximately three weeks and then to exchange reports about the experiences. The authors looked at what phenomena elicited these emotions as they went about their daily routines: seeing a baby smile, students playing table tennis, the branches of a tree that bend toward a river. For example, one of the authors was walking on a beach when his attention fell on a small swale filled with seawater, and observing the play of light in the water, he described his inner experience as follows:

> I experience an intense tenderness towards the phenomenon—the wish not to interfere with it, to let it be as it is, let it express itself [. . .]. The sense of being touched. There is a remarkable sense of gratitude to be in a position to observe and experience this. A silence, a joy, a sense of inner jubilation; a respect towards the magic of nature. A bliss in taking note of this delicate subtlety. I want to make sure not to tell someone about it who is not prepared and could talk it down. An inner sense of expansion and forgetting mundane trivialities.[41]

The authors note that merely being mindful of these emotions and seeking them out deliberately already increased the frequency of experiencing them. Awe and wonder could not be triggered on the spot or deliberately called forth, and yet, "it was as though we were in a position to contribute to the stage on which the phenomenon of awe and wonder occurred through this more deliberate and intensified attention."[42] Perhaps religion as wonder-technology does this: it opens the mind for experiences that elicit awe and wonder.

As we saw in the previous chapter, stage magicians try to force an experience of wonder. With religious practices, you do not force yourself to experience wonder, but you can cultivate certain ways of engaging with the world that make you more receptive to wonder. This can work by using language that invokes explicit reference to awe and wonder, as is common in hymns or even in simple liturgical phrases, such as, "Great is the mystery of faith."

Material culture can also elicit these emotions. For example, the spatial dimensions of religious architecture can evoke a sense of awe. Monumental religious architecture is cross-culturally widespread, ranging from buildings such as Hagia Sophia in Istanbul (built as the patriarchal cathedral of the imperial capital of the Byzantine Empire), the splendors and intricacies of the Hindu temples in Angkor Vat, Cambodia, and European gothic cathedrals that were built ever airier and higher, such as Cologne Cathedral. Part of the explanation for this drive for height is costly signaling: making buildings tall requires know-how and resources and thus signals the wealth of the patron in charge of the project.[43] However, massive buildings also exploit our sensory responses to vastness. We saw in chapter 3 how awe is typically experienced in response to something vast, whether physical or conceptual. Height and spaciousness in buildings elicit a sense of awe in people who visit them.[44]

Other forms of religious awe-technology are not physical, but instead work through embodied practices that train us to see the world differently. Mindfulness practices such as the blessings Heschel mentions are widespread, and serve as a cognitive wonder-technology. Take the ubiquitous use of "expedient means" or "pedagogy" (*upāya*) in Chan/Zen Buddhism. These are a variety of religious cognitive techniques that are aimed at helping the practitioner realize that the Buddha-nature is emptiness. *Upāya* include ephemeral and sometimes banal practices such as gardening, doing household chores, sand painting, pondering kōans (a kind of riddle), and martial arts. Zen Buddhists teach that, to reach enlightenment, we need to realize that the self is an illusion. The idea of a Buddha-nature explains how it is possible that all sentient beings, in a successive cycle of rebirths, can attain the state of a Buddha. There are no lowly and high things; rather, everything is part of the same fabric of reality. The Buddha-nature is also empty of an independent, individual, and substantial self. Realizing these truths—and thus achieving enlightenment—is not something you only do intellectually, by studying texts. In Zen Buddhism, this happens through *upāya,* embodied practices where you experience these truths. Because the idea of no-self and the lack of distinction between high and low things is so counterintuitive, we need to abandon heuristic frameworks and preconceived ideas of the nature of reality. In this process of abandonment, wonder is a useful technology.

Kōans, riddles that are given to Zen monk novices, serve as a wonder-technology. The novice has to consider the kōan and come up with some answer. From this answer, the more advanced monks can gauge how far he understands a particular concept. For example, the famous kōan that asks about the sound of one hand clapping probes how far the novice understands the concept of non-duality. Pondering kōans requires a shift in thinking, a shift away from the everyday to what may lie underneath the mundane. Here are three examples, two of which involve the Chinese Buddhist Chan master Zhaozhou Congshen (778–897):

> Master Zhaozhou was asked by a monk, "Does a dog have the Buddha-nature or does it not have it?"

Zhaozhou said, "It has nothing." [*Wu* (nothing) could also be translated as "emptiness," insofar as everything is characterized by emptiness, by not having an individual self. This is the first kōan traditionally assigned to a novice monk in a Chan/Zen Buddhist temple.]

A monk asked, "What is Buddha?"

Master Yunmen replied, "A dried shit-stick." [A shit-stick is the functional equivalent of toilet paper.][45]

(Content warning: I cannot guarantee that no cats were harmed in the formulation of the following kōan.)

When the monks of the Western and Eastern Halls were quarreling over a cat, Master Nanquan held it up and said, "If you are able to speak, I will spare it; if you cannot speak, I will kill it." No one could answer, so Nanquan proceeded to kill the cat.

That evening Zhaozhou returned from afar, and Nanquan told him what had happened. Zhaozhou took off one sandal, put it on his head, and left. Nanquan said, "If you had been there, you would have saved the cat." [The novice is here invited to consider why putting the sandal on one's head would have saved the cat; a pointless gesture, perhaps indicating emptiness.][46]

Kōans do not spell out a clear answer and often rely on shock or surprise. By doing so, they encourage reflection by the reader and a change of attitude. Chan/Zen Buddhists believe that a sudden surprise could help you to realize the emptiness behind everything.

Karesansui, the Japanese dry garden, is another form of *upāya*, and another wonder-technology. Literally, *kare san sui* can be translated as "dry-mountain-water," evoking the idea of water without actual water. In the West these gardens are called Zen gardens; they are often part of the layout of a botanical garden. These landscapes are not meant to be walked in, but to be gazed at and contemplated. Julianne Chung argues that they are meant to help to bring about a personal transformation in onlookers, to help them become ecological citizens.[47] It is by being immersed in the contemplation of the garden that the visitor can get a phenomenological sense of the importance of the balance between herself and the world, that she depends on her environment, and should strive to live in harmony with it. Thus, Japanese dry landscapes constitute a kind of non-verbal moral testimony: they teach the viewer something morally important, but they do it non-verbally, without explicit instruction. Chung discusses the following anecdote by Robert Carter about his visiting Ryoan-ji, a well-known *karesansui* in Kyoto:

> Once, after having just come from several hours at the garden's side, I was welcomed into the home of the distinguished Zen Buddhist philosopher, Nishitani Keiji, in Kyoto. He asked where I was coming from, and when I told him about my visit to Ryoan-ji, he quickly asked whether I had heard the garden roar. Zen gardens are, supposedly, so authentic in their dry waterfalls and dry riverbeds that a keen listener can hear the roar of the water. On a later visit to his home, he returned to Ryoan-ji as a topic, and this time further elaborated that most people who visit the great landscape gardens merely "look at the surface [. . . ,] at the beautiful rocks, the rippled patterns in the sand, the moss, and the earth-colored walls. But the garden is the expression of the landscape architect's own enlightenment! [. . .] Underneath our feet [if we imagine ourselves back at Ryoan-ji], where we are, at this place, the garden is looking at us, for we are now a part of the

> actual manifestation of the garden architect's own enlightenment experience. The garden is my Zen master now, and it is your Zen master, too." The garden can be a source of our own personal self-transformation, if we will let it, for it is an expression of the self-transformation of the master architect. It is so much more than a simple selection of interesting stones, cleverly arranged, like a paper collage.[48]

In a classic monograph on memory and religion, the anthropologist Harvey Whitehouse distinguishes between two modes of religiosity, the imagistic and the doctrinal.[49] The imagistic mode involves emotionally charged, infrequent rituals. They're often painful and uncomfortable, involving such elements as hunger, thirst, and physical alteration (e.g., scarification and circumcision). Their memory is episodic (personal and autobiographical) and lasts a lifetime, often as a "flashbulb memory." Such rituals help to fuse the identity of the practitioner with the wider group. The doctrinal mode consists, however, of smaller, quieter, unspectacular rituals that are performed frequently. For example, celebrating the Eucharist weekly does not give lasting memories of the event, but employs semantic and procedural memory (about how the ritual goes). The doctrinal mode also helps people fuse their identities, but alters them in a less radical way than do rituals in the imagistic mode.

And yet, using the tools offered by Merleau-Ponty, we can see that religious rituals that are low-arousal nevertheless can have a marked effect, and can be personally transformative. This transformation doesn't happen in one fell swoop as in the imagistic mode. Rather, it happens gradually while we train ourselves into new habits. These habits change how we see the world and make us engage with it differently.[50] Religious rituals are conducive to wonder, because they subvert our everyday way of doing things. They are patterned ways in which we deliberately shape and transform our actions. Ritual actions consist of doing things whereby we "subject ourselves to externally given categories of order."[51] For example, a simple ritualistic action is removing one's shoes upon entering a house. When we engage others in the mode of ritual, we subject ourselves to an externally imposed order, a way of doing things that doesn't originate within us. Because it is imposed and dictated by a script or a tradition, a tension with the real world arises. By engaging in ritual, we create an "as if" world, a world of pretense and imagination where things are different from how they are in our everyday environment. This tension gives freedom to see things again as if for the first time. By taking off your shoes when entering a house, you show that you realize a home is a place that is set apart of a society, though it is also part of it. Homes can have their own rules and behaviors, which can be different from those of society at large. Maybe this can force you to think about how homes differ from societies, and how you might want society to resemble home more. Taking off your shoes is a sign of embodied respect for what lies within the home, the environment where people can sit together for a meal and have a harmonious discussion.

We can thus envisage a more modest and a more ambitious thesis about how religion harnesses awe and wonder. A more modest hypothesis, which I have set out here, says that some religious practices can help us see with firstness: that is, to recover a sense of wonder at the world and to rid ourselves of complacency. These practices are aimed at questioning how we engage normally with the world. They allow practitioners to put themselves in deliberate tension with how the world is. Examples include blessings in Judaism and *upāya* in Buddhism. A more ambitious thesis would hold that wonder is central to religious practices. Rituals (both religious and non-religious) are in deliberate tension with our ordinary experience and help us to enter a liminal in-between space of ritual ambiguity. I haven't given enough reason to think this more ambitious hypothesis is correct. Religion is a multifaceted and diverse phenomenon of human experience; no single silver-bullet explanation will adequately capture it.

Closing this chapter, we can see how religious awe- and wonder-technology can be liberating. It can free us from seeing the world in certain set ways, allowing us to meet the wondrousness of the world we are part of on its own terms. Religious practices that aim at wonder afford a kind of freedom in their limitations. We don't need to think about how meditation, mindfulness, or kōans make us more productive—engaging with these practices for that reason would be contrary to their aims. Rather, in pursuing them we can begin to question the idea of productivity, and what role it plays in our collective lives.

6

Cabinet of Wonders

HOW AWE AND WONDER REGULATE SCIENCE

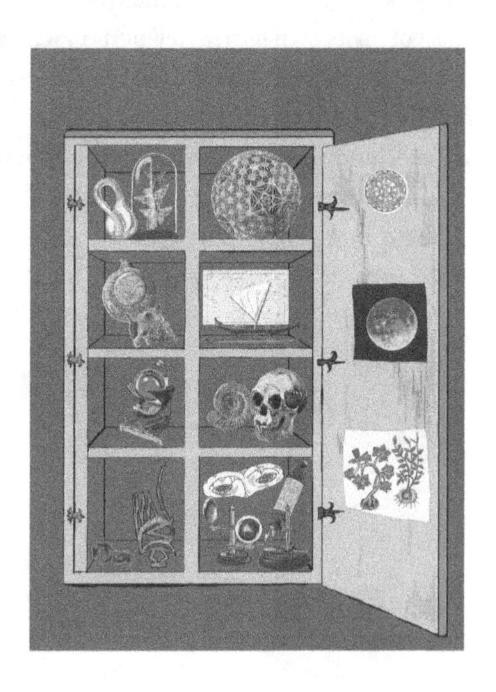

Is Ball Lightning Real? And How Could We Tell?

Aside from grim descriptions of living under Nazi rule in Belgium during World War II, my grandparents had fascinating and magnificent stories to tell. In particular, they told of a mysterious phenomenon: ball lightning. If you opened the window while a thunderstorm was brewing, a tight crackling ball of lightning might fly into your house. You would then need to sit all still and quiet, and hope the ball lightning would leave from where it came. Once, my grandmother and her sisters and parents were listening to the radio in their sitting room when a lightning ball swept into the house, rolled around over the carpet, and then made its way back out through the same window. In the mid-twentieth century, eyewitness reports of this phenomenon were so common that it featured as a plot device in Hergé's Tintin album *Les Sept Boules de cristal* (*The Seven Crystal Balls*), published in 1948. There are thousands of reports of this elusive meteorological phenomenon, but as yet no conclusive scientific explanation, though some progress has been made this century.[1] Until the 1970s, it was unclear whether ball lightning even existed. Along with many other people, I doubted testimonies such as my grandparents', though they were deeply practical folk, not given to flights of fancy.

Ball lightning is part of a bigger picture, in which nature is not always well-behaved and predictable, but capricious and unknowable. When should we trust a report of a strange phenomenon and when should we dismiss it? This methodological question vexed early modern scientists who tried to come to grips with "strange facts." Early scientific accounts from the late sixteenth and early seventeenth centuries are replete with them: a girl with horns growing on her body, several suns observed simultaneously, conjoined twins.[2] Some of these still feature in experimental kits for children: unusual chemical reactions, magnetism, light fractured through prisms. An early impetus to this collection of strange facts is the "cabinet of curiosity" or *Wunderkammer* (from the German; "wonder room"), also called "cabinet of wonders." Such collections of strange objects and marvelous oddities were cataloged and individually framed in whatever assortment the collector saw fit. They were meant to be marveled at. They could be fossils, artifacts brought home by explorers from distant lands, old trinkets; a mix of art and artifice. Whereas contemporary natural history museums are neat and tidy, arranging objects by type and Linnaean classification, these collections were assemblages of whatever struck their owners as strange or charming. We get a sense of their diversity from this random selection from the catalog of the Anatomie-Hall of the University of Leiden (in the Netherlands), first published in the late sixteenth century, which went through numerous new editions (this one is from 1723)[3]:

36. The Covering of a great Mumie upon which is engraven the Effigies of Ceres.
37. A Young Elephant's Head.
38. An Unknown Sea Fish.
39. A Sea Hedg hog.
40. The Sceleton of a Lapwing.

Cabinets of curiosity were later replaced by the systematic collections we see in contemporary natural history museums, although there are still people making them today. I spoke with Hester Loeff, a Dutch maker of cabinets of curiosity, who considers herself—as an amateur and not a professional scientist—to be an heir to the tradition.[4] She is conservator of the collection "naturalia" (natural objects) of the Royal Zeeland Scientific Society, a Dutch scientific society founded in 1769. Crafting cabinets of curiosity with traditional techniques, her collections continue to elicit a sense of wonder in her customers. Among many things, her cabinets contain individually bottled sand from deserts across the world, a mouse fetus kept preserved in bioethanol, an ancient flint spearpoint from Niger, and fossils collected on North Sea beaches that she finds while beachcombing. By resisting the systemizing of the contemporary natural sciences, she aims to help the people who purchase her cabinets to reclaim their sense of wonder. To her, the connection between science, knowledge, and wonder is intimate, but increasing scientific specialization and distance from the public makes this hard to see—science used to be fun and exciting, but now is aloof and intimidating.

This chapter discusses the relationship between science and our sense of awe and wonder. I build on ideas of early modern authors such as Descartes and Smith to get a clearer picture of this relationship. Unlike magic, science is not a cognitive technology that aims to produce wonders. Yet, it crucially depends on our sense of awe and wonder. The relationship between science and wonder is dynamic. Scientists wish to articulate the wondrous, but one of the aims of science is ultimately to diagram and systemize it, thereby making it intelligible. Once we have a satisfying account of a given phenomenon, our sense of wonder fades and ceases. This, at any rate, is how Descartes conceived of wonder and its role in science. As we have seen, he thought that wonder was useful for scientific inquiry, but that once we get a picture of the laws of nature, it is appropriate to cease wondering. By contrast, Smith believed that whenever we devise new theories, there are new opportunities for anomalies to arise, and so, new opportunities for wonder. What happens when scientists are confronted with so many anomalies that their theories don't work any more? Drawing on Jean-Paul Sartre's theory of the emotions, I argue that they use awe and wonder to give anomalies their proper due, and to construct new theories.

Of Marvels and Miracles

Medieval people were not as gullible as we often assume. As a matter of fact, sometimes they were too skeptical. For example, scholars only accepted reports of stones raining down from the sky (meteorites) in the eighteenth century, though shepherds and other country folk who were out at night frequently observed them and picked them up after impact. Medieval natural philosophers and early scientists took pains to dismiss these reports. Meteorites were part of folklore. Norwegian peasants attributed supernatural powers to them: placing a meteorite close to a woman in labor would aid delivery.[5]

In the later Middle Ages, many towns and cities claimed to have a saint's relic with alleged miraculous properties. While these claims may have their roots in sincere devotion and ritual, they were at least partly driven by financial calculations. A relic would attract pilgrims, who would boost the local economy in a way not dissimilar from attracting tourists today. To stop a wild proliferation of shrines and saints, church officials sought to separate "genuine" miracles from mere natural processes, questioning eyewitnesses in situ. In this way the Catholic church imposed stringent criteria to distinguish "genuine" miracles from false reports, or from marvels.

Medieval philosophers distinguished between marvels and miracles, *mirabilia* and *miracula*. The former were natural occurrences they did not understand, such as a two-headed calf, magnetism, or unusual chemical reactions. Some authors equated marvels with natural magic (as we saw, this is how Giordano Bruno referred to it). Natural magic is that part of magic that belongs to the workings of nature and does not have a supernatural, such as a demonic or divine, origin. Natural magicians such as John Dee frequently had to defend themselves against charges that their magic was demonic. So, rather paradoxically, perhaps, for contemporary readers, they insisted that their magic was entirely natural.[6] The common perception at the time was that marvels could be the work of demons. Miracles, by contrast, came from God, who caused nature to behave in unusual ways.[7] The psychological reaction to marvels and miracles was the same: *admiratio*; that is, awe and wonder. How to distinguish between the marvelous and the miraculous, if they appear the same to us? In his *Letter to a Certain Knight beyond the Mountains on the Occult Workings of Nature*, the theologian Thomas Aquinas (1225–1274) discussed instances of natural magic (the tides, magnets) and the question of how to distinguish them from miracles, such as the workings of relics. Aquinas believed that to distinguish natural magic from miracles, we should use conceptual, theological tools. It would never have entered his mind to say that conducting experiments would be a way to do this.[8]

In Aquinas's time, natural philosophers who worked in the Aristotelian tradition in the halls of universities such as Oxford, Paris, and Bologna did not conduct experiments. Their interest did not lie in the exceptional, but in the regular: in how nature behaves normally. Their elegant models could explain a wide range of phenomena, such as the retrograde motion of the planets (as part of the Ptolemaic picture of the universe), or the ecological relationships between different kinds of organisms (the *scala naturae*, or great chain of being). There was no place for wonder in these models. This is why, as Augustine had already observed, the distinction between what is and isn't a marvel is to some extent subjective.[9] The eclipse which elicits awe and wonder in a peasant is not marvelous to an astronomer, who predicted its advent and who has a picture of the world that explains why eclipses occur.

As we saw in chapter 4, Renaissance magicians and alchemists differed from natural philosophers in their attention to the wondrous. Rather than dismissing strange facts as inconvenient for their elegant pictures of the natural world, they embraced them. They would focus intensely on them, conducting experiments to replicate their occurrence. Early modern science inherited this focus on the particular. Natural philosophy was "smooth," focused on regularities and skimming over strange and inconvenient facts. By contrast, early modern science was "grainy"—that is, "full of experiential particulars conspicuously detached from explanatory or theoretical moorings."[10]

The English philosopher and statesman Francis Bacon (1561–1626) is an exemplar of early modern science and its method. He recommended that a scientist should do his best to collect a broad sampling of observations, including ones that were strange and unexpected. This attention to anomalies helps to guard against confirmation bias. Bacon borrowed elements from the magical tradition to develop his scientific method.[11] This reversed the natural philosophical method of first making a model, and then checking whether it coheres with the regular workings of nature. Bacon's method goes from particular observations to the general. We start out looking at particular phenomena, not just nature well-behaved but also nature ill-behaved, and then see if we can distill a theory that is both more general and more precise.

To give a sense of the enormous difficulty in this Baconian endeavor, consider an early modern scientist who tries to gauge the efficacy of weapon salve. Weapon salve was a form of natural magic developed by the Swiss physician Paracelsus in the sixteenth century. When a person was hurt by a weapon, an ointment that could cure wounds was applied to the offending weapon. Meanwhile, the wound itself was kept clean and lightly dressed. Above all, the weapon salve should not touch the wound directly. Reliable and repeated observation showed that weapon salve worked better than traditional medicine, which was applied directly to the wound. Sometimes (indeed often, on a battlefield) the weapon was no longer available for this treatment. No problem: the salve worked equally well when applied to a bandage that had been blood-stained by the wound, as long as the wound itself was not touched by the salve.[12] What explains the efficacy of weapon salve? A quick look at ointments used in these days brings clarification. Ointments were laced with polluted substances such as egg-shells and feathers to encourage the wound to form pus, which physicians mistakenly thought was a required part of the healing process. Obviously, it is better not to pollute a wound and to keep it clean than to apply treatments that contribute to festering and other unhygienic practices. This explains why wounds deliberately not treated with salves and ointments did better than wounds treated the traditional way. The experimental method at the time clearly vindicated natural magic in the form of weapon salve, but only because it is better just to keep a wound clean than to smear unclean substances on it. The fact that the salve was smeared on the offending weapon was irrelevant. (In the absence of double-blind tests with a control condition, this was unclear to contemporaries.)

Observations and intellectual contributions from outside Western culture played a critical role in the scientific revolution. Medieval maps were drawn and scaled with *terra incognita,* on which prowled wondrous beasts. As Europeans came increasingly into contact with people in the New World, Africa, and Asia, and later on also Australia and the Pacific, they witnessed a wealth of botanical, astronomical, and zoological observations that to them were wondrous. These were collected into motley cabinets of wonders, and detailed in *cosmographiae*, which mapped out the world in all its wild diversity. Highlighting particular facts, including strange ones, they had a crucial influence upon early modern science.

As historian of science James Poskett details, this influence of insights and data from outside of Europe was not just a one-way process, whereby European explorers and settlers went to look at the local vegetation, animals, and geography.[13] Rather, European scholars relied on the findings and observations of Indigenous people who had clear systems of botanical and other forms of knowledge. For example, Martín de la Cruz, a Nahua (Aztec) herbal physician wrote a book on herbal medicine in 1552, the first to appear in the Americas. It is a beautifully illustrated volume, containing Indigenous botanical knowledge, which was translated into Latin.[14] The way this book was organized and illustrated was influential for later European herbal medicine.

European early modern map-making and navigation also drew significantly on the expertise of Indigenous people. For example, James Cook's chief navigator on HMS *Endeavour* was an Indigenous Tahitian priest, Tupaia (ca. 1725–1770), who was an expert on star sea navigation (the technique is detailed in chapter 3). The map Tupaia drew of the Pacific was enormous and detailed, containing over seventy islands, an area equivalent to the size of the entire contiguous United States. He combined European conventions such as lines of longitude and latitude with Polynesian nautical principles, such as directions for bearing, and representing traveling time between islands, which was significantly affected by prevailing currents and winds. Cook used this map to navigate the Pacific Ocean successfully. It had a lasting influence on cartography and European knowledge of Oceania after it was mass-printed.[15] We should think of the rise of early modern science not as an internal European process, but as a syncretic and multifaceted global phenomenon.

Thus, European exploration and colonization had a deep impact on science and what sorts of empirical observations were admissible. It was no longer possible to ignore the data from far-flung places, or the observations of a wide range of people. A disturbing idea took shape: most of what the ancients believed, and so most of European medieval knowledge, was wrong! The botanical collection of Martín de la Cruz did not fit the European pre-Linnaean taxonomy. The Pacific Ocean was not some barren waterscape, but a detailed terrain consisting of many islands, currents, winds, and reefs.

Early modern scientists strove to make a picture of nature that was both more precise and more general, so that it could accommodate the wondrous and the previously unknown. From Descartes onward, we see more talk about God as a divine legislator, who promulgates laws of nature. The picture of the divine legislator was fruitful because it conceived of laws of nature in two ways: on the one hand, the laws always hold, without exception, because God can impose the divine will on nature with absoluteness. Any object in the proximity of the earth will be attracted to it (and vice versa), for example, because gravity always works. On the other hand, God could freely decide what to do and what nature should look like. The laws of nature could have been very different, if God had chosen to make them so.[16] The mind of God is elusive and cannot be grasped by human reason. So, we cannot solely rely on reason to discern the laws of nature. We need observations and reliable reports. This means we should accept the marvels; we can't gloss over weird facts, because they matter to us as valuable data. If weapon salve seems to work better than ointments applied to wounds, and if stones rain out of the sky, there must be a natural explanation for why this is so.

While natural magic was absorbed into early modern science, miracles became increasingly more difficult to make sense of. If the laws of nature hold everywhere, without exception, how can we conceive of miracles? It is only at this point, sometime in the late seventeenth to early eighteenth century, that our current view of miracles became popular: miracles violate the laws of nature. Because the laws of nature do not have exceptions (at least not in our experience), the concept of miracle became inherently unstable.[17] A miracle is a violation of the laws of nature. But the laws of nature are inviolable because they were stipulated by God, who never makes a mistake. Thus, reports of miracles have a low probability of being true.[18] In this way, modern science squeezed miracles out of existence. Did it also snuff out the marvelous? The answer to this question is not obvious, and is of enduring interest.

Does Science Cause Us to Lose a Sense of Wonder?

Science communicator Richard Dawkins is best known as a fierce critic of religion, but he is also deeply spiritual. Indeed, as Eric Steinhart has argued, throughout his work Dawkins outlines a spiritual naturalism, offering the vision of a world that we can wonder at and stand in awe of, filled with hope and joy.[19] The foundation for his spiritual naturalism is science. In striking contrast to Heschel, who believed that the scientific attitude leads to a loss of wonder, Dawkins proclaims that awe and wonder are part and parcel of the scientific attitude. In *Unweaving the Rainbow,* Dawkins addresses the English poet John Keats's suggestion that Newton "destroyed the poetry of the rainbow by reducing it to a prism," and that natural philosophy (which meant science in that context) had unwoven the rainbow by analyzing it to death.[20]

Not so, says Dawkins. His central claim in *Unweaving the Rainbow* is that "the spirit of wonder which led Blake to Christian mysticism, Keats to Arcadian myth and Yeats to Fenians and fairies, is the very same spirit that moves great scientists."[21] For Dawkins, science can take the place of religion as a wonder-technology, and is even superior in that respect:

> The great religions have a place for awe, for ecstatic transport at the wonder and beauty of creation. And it's exactly this feeling of spine-shivering, breath-catching awe—almost worship—this flooding of the chest with epiphanic wonder, that modern science can provide. And it does so beyond the wildest dreams of saints and mystics. The fact that the supernatural has no place in our explanations, in our understanding of the universe and life, doesn't diminish the awe.[22]

For people who know Dawkins primarily as an unrelenting critic of religion, these remarks may seem surprising. For example, the theologian Celia Deane-Drummond remarks, "Even Richard Dawkins, that *bête noir* of the religious community, admits to wonder through science."[23] However, there is no incoherence in Dawkins's position. Atheism does not entail the absence of awe and wonder.

The theoretical physicist Richard Feynman (1918–1988), a self-avowed atheist, likewise held that understanding and knowledge are no obstacles to wonder:

> Poets say that science takes away from the beauty of the stars—mere globs of gas atoms. Nothing is "mere." I too can

> see the stars on a desert night, and feel them. But do I see less or more? The vastness of the heavens stretches my imagination—stuck on this carousel my little eye can catch one-million-year-old light. A vast pattern—of which I am a part—perhaps my stuff was belched from some forgotten star, as one is belching there. Or see them with the greater eye of Palomar, rushing all apart from some common starting point when they were perhaps all together. What is the pattern, or the meaning, or the *why*? It does not do harm to the mystery to know a little about it. For far more marvelous is the truth than any artist of the past imagined![24]

Wonder lies at the edge of knowing; it opens vistas to the unknown by directing our attention to it. Feynman, like Dawkins, protests that science doesn't unweave the rainbow, because there are always new things to be discovered, in line with Adam Smith's view. As we saw in chapter 3, there was a major discussion on whether lack of knowledge is a core aspect of the sublime (which we can see as a kind of awe), with Kant maintaining there must be some things we don't know in order to experience the sublime, and Herder maintaining that more knowledge can be conducive to awe. Unresolved philosophical questions and perplexities continue to surround even things we are confident about, such as the existence of vacua. Hence, as Dawkins and Feynman argue, science doesn't unweave the rainbow. On the contrary, our understanding of how rainbows are physically realized opens new mysteries, such as about the structure of color, and of reality itself.

Still, the relationship between science and awe and wonder requires elucidation. One way to flesh this out, which I believe is implicit in much of Dawkins's writings, is that science allows us to *see* more wondrous things. You don't need science to appreciate the beauty of nature. We often have a visceral and immediate response to natural beauty, even without background knowledge. When I was twelve years old, I visited Malaysia, the country my father grew up in. We stayed on a small island in the archipelago of Langkawi. In the 1990s, tourism was only beginning there, and the islands still had intact rainforest with mysterious flowers blooming in its depths, and natural waterfalls. To accommodate the early tourists, bamboo bridges and paths were constructed so we could walk easily without hurting ourselves or getting stung or bitten by insects too much (we were only stung a little bit, but twelve-year-old me thought it was a lot). Though the surroundings were very humid and uncomfortable, I still vividly recall my wonder at the astounding beauty of these islands, at seeing large hornbills hop from branch to branch, or the sudden vivid pink of an orchid against deep green foliage. Yet, I was not aware of the ecological relationships of hornbills, orchids, and trees. We can be moved by the grandeur of a waterfall, the elegance of a hornbill, the striking contrast of an orchid and its dark surroundings. Since we are part of nature, we are always part of the scenes we are contemplating. We are immersed by virtue of being embodied. Such experiences are multisensory: light filters through the trees, rain gushes down in a sudden outburst and then evaporates just as quickly, leaving a refreshing smell. This embodied, participatory experience allows us to wonder at nature without being botanists or ecologists.

However, this leaves open the possibility that knowledge can *enhance* our experiences of nature. If a botanist had made the same trip as twelve-year-old me, they would have seen plants and their relationships that eluded (and would still elude) me. Their enhanced understanding affords opportunities for differentiated wonder. Allen Carlson, an influential voice in environmental aesthetics, holds that scientific knowledge of the natural world is a vital aspect of nature appreciation.[25] Perhaps we can see Dawkinsian wonder as a way of looking at the world that science affords and that would not be possible without it. Consider Dawkins's example of the hidden depths of the ocean:

> We can recapture that sense of having just tumbled out to life on a new world by looking at our own world in unfamiliar ways. It's tempting to use an easy example like a rose or a butterfly, but let's go straight for the alien deep end. I remember attending a lecture, years ago, by a biologist working on octopuses, and their relatives the squids and cuttlefish. He began by explaining his fascination with these animals. "You see," he said, "they are the Martians." Have you ever watched a squid change color?[26]

Adam Smith's discussion of wonder in his *History of Astronomy,* which we examined in chapter 2, helps us to make further sense of this. Our sense of wonder at anomalous data, such as an unexpected eclipse or a strange plant, encourages us to create scientific explanations in which these phenomena find a place. For example, in 1862 Darwin was sent a specimen of an orchid with a deep calyx (*Angraecum sesquipedale*), and he predicted the existence of a moth with an unfathomably long tongue (of 25–30 cm) that would be able to extract the nectar; Alfred Russel Wallace, co-discoverer of evolutionary theory, also predicted this. That moth was only discovered in 1903, and was called *Xanthopan morganii praedicta,* "the predicted one".[27]

Once we are able to categorize, our sense of wonder declines, but at the same time, we become more alert to potential new marvels. In the sections that follow, I present the case of paradigm change, whereby scientists harness their sense of awe and wonder to rid themselves of schemas that no longer work for them. Wonder becomes a way for scientists to get unstuck.

Awe and Wonder in Paradigm Changes

When a scientific paradigm breaks down, scientists need to make a leap into the unknown.[28] These are moments of revolution, as identified by historian of science Thomas Kuhn, when a scientific worldview becomes untenable and the agreed-upon and accepted truths of a particular discipline are radically called into question.[29] Beloved theories are revealed to have been built upon sand. Explanations that held up for hundreds of years are dismissed. A particular and productive way of looking at the world turns out to be erroneous. Scientific revolutions—such as those instigated by Copernicus, Newton, Lavoisier, Darwin, or Wegener—are times of great uncertainty, when cool, disinterested reason alone doesn't help scientists move forward, because so many of their usual assumptions turn out to be flawed.

Take geologists and the shift to the idea of continental drift. A mere hundred years ago, the idea that continents move was a minority position. This view was termed "mobilism," and it was contrasted with the dominant "fixist" idea. According to the latter, landmasses are, as they appear to be, immobile. An early proponent of mobilism was meteorologist and polar explorer Alfred Wegener. Going against an overwhelming scientific consensus, which was shaped by Charles Lyell and other early geologists, Wegener proposed that during the Carboniferous period all continents were united in what he called "Pangaea," a single supercontinent. In 1912 Wegener presented some evidence: for example, how the coastlines of West Africa and eastern South America fit together like a jigsaw puzzle, and fossil evidence of closely related animals that appeared to live in places that were wide apart, but that once lived in adjacent regions.[30] His theory was mostly met with ridicule. Then, so a popular scientific myth goes, scientists were presented with an overwhelming amount of evidence for mobilism, as well as a plausible mechanism behind it—namely, plate tectonics. This helped scientists rationally to conclude that mobilism is correct, and that fixism ought to be rejected. In a short span of time, the vast majority of geologists and geophysicists adopted the mobilist view, in the form of plate tectonics, which they still hold today. This story emphasizes the rationality of scientists and their sensitivity to evidence. Science goes where the evidence points.

The actual history of this paradigm shift is more complicated. As science sociologist Pablo Pellegrini details, Wegener was part of a minority tradition, but he was not the only mobilist.[31] We also see mobilist ideas among his contemporaries Frank Bursley Taylor, Roberto Mantovani, and Eduard Suess. Mobilism can be traced further back still. In 1801 Alexander von Humboldt proposed a supercontinent based on the shape of the current continents, and we see even earlier mobilist ideas in Buffon, Lamarck, and others. The earliest author to voice this idea was Abraham Ortelius (1527–1598), a Brabantian cartographer who created the first modern atlas; noticing how the continents fit together he proposed they were torn apart by earthquakes and floods. These theories differed in important details, such as the shape of the ancient hypothetical supercontinent and the cause of its breaking apart.

Nevertheless, mobilism was a minority position until well into the 1960s.[32] Its adoption in its contemporary incarnation of plate tectonics first gained support slowly, but then more rapidly, and within twenty years' time (by the late 1970s/early 1980s), the shift was complete. If scientists were not solely persuaded by a sufficient amount of evidence, what explains paradigm shifts like these? Also, what persuades scientists to accept some phenomena, such as meteorites and (increasingly) ball lightning, as genuine? Why do they remain skeptical of others, such as UFOs as potential evidence for extraterrestrial life?

Philosopher of science Bas van Fraassen notes that a decision to accept a new paradigm and abandon the old one is not an entirely rational process: "some people are beginning to talk about a strange new theory that makes absolutely no sense and violates the most basic commonsensical expectations of what nature can be like."[33] The motivation for giving the new theory consideration is that the old theory suffers from increasingly many anomalies: observations that don't fit what it predicts. As these anomalies begin to proliferate, scientists have to decide. Should they go on as before, becoming ever more burdened by anomalies and an increasingly sterile existing paradigm, or should they adopt a new conceptual framework that challenges their most deeply held convictions? Even as anomalies accumulate, sticking with the old paradigm is usually the rational choice (if only for career reasons), while going with the new, unfamiliar hypotheses—not yet crystallized into a new paradigm—is, on the face of it, not easy to justify.[34] Accepting the emerging paradigm is a leap of faith, not knowing where you might land. In this leap, emotions play a crucial role.

Jean-Paul Sartre on the Emotions

Bas van Fraassen argues that making rational decisions cannot help scientists when they decide to accept an emerging paradigm or decide to leave the sinking ship: because the strange new theory does not make sense to them, they cannot take a rational course of action.[35] Rather, they need radically to shift their attitude, changing themselves to some extent, so as to accommodate the new information. How can they accomplish this shift? To answer this question, van Fraassen draws on

Jean-Paul Sartre's *Sketch for a Theory of the Emotions* (*Esquisse d'une theorie des émotions*, 1939).[36] Using Sartre's framework, he argues that emotions can help scientists to transform themselves, and in this way, help them to deal with fundamental shifts in scientific understanding. Emotions can help them to value a new paradigm which may seem on the face of it not entirely intelligible, or even absurd.

The French existentialist and phenomenologist Jean-Paul Sartre (1905–1980) formulated his theory of the emotions in response to the major theories at the time, in particular William James and Pierre Janet's emotional behavioral theory and Sigmund Freud's psychoanalytic theory of emotions. Both theories treat emotions as passive states—as things that happen to you (as is clear in phrases like "falling in love", or "being gripped with jealousy"). Sartre, by contrast, held that emotions are things we *do*. They have a goal, and they are intentional: that is, they are actions we carry out deliberately. Because of this, we are responsible for our emotions. For example, when we get angry, we do so to seek a solution, to resolve a tense situation.

> When the paths before us become too difficult, or when we cannot see our way, we can no longer put up with such an exacting and difficult world. All ways are barred and nevertheless we must act. So then we try to change the world.[37]

Emotions are a way for us to bestow values, to direct our attention, to care about things in our environment.[38] The world Sartre refers to is the world of our subjective experiences. It is the world of our needs, fears, and hopes. In Sartre's view, the way emotions help us transform the world is akin to magic: a magical act alters the attitude of the practitioner to the world. We do not change *the* world, but we do change *our* world, by shifting our needs, fears, and hopes through emotions that help us to value or devalue certain elements in it.[39] Take Sartre's example of sour grapes: seeing that the grapes are out of reach, you decide, "they are too sour anyway." While the chemical properties of the grapes haven't changed, you have altered how they taste for you. In this way, the world has become a bit more bearable. Anticipating contemporary ideas about embodied cognition, Sartre speculated that physical actions help us to produce emotions. We clench our fists in anger. We weep in sadness. Thus, the conflict is resolved.

Sartre's sketch presents an alternative to William James, who argued that physiological states (such as weeping) are prior to the felt affect (such as feeling sad), and that they are involuntary.[40] Rather, Sartre prefigures ideas about embodied cognition in arguing we actively produce emotions as a way to resolve a situation, an impasse we find ourselves in. Weeping is like an incantation that causes us to feel sad, and that in turn gives rise to a different perspective on the world. All of a sudden everything looks bleak, taking the sting out of what made us sad in the first place. The difference between Sartre and James is that it is for Sartre the *agent* who initiates the weeping—the Sartrean agent is not overcome or gripped by it, but is in control of it. When we weep, our act is sincere, and we initiate it. Sartre presupposes that we have direct control over our emotions. However, we engage in practices (cognitive technologies) that over time help to shape how we respond emotionally to a variety of situations. Thus, it's more likely that we have indirect control over our emotions.

Awe and Scientific Understanding

Applying Sartre's account of emotions to scientific practice, van Fraassen argues that scientists draw on their emotions when dealing with new, bewildering ideas, especially those that sprout up during scientific revolutions. If the paradigm they work in is faltering, they need to change the way they view the world—and this requires changing their emotions, and thereby changing their world. They need to transform both who they are and what they know. Only when scientists themselves are transformed can they accept a theory that they originally thought outlandish or ridiculous. In this way, van Fraassen integrates the important role of emotions in scientific practice.

At first blush, this picture is attractive, but it needs some filling out. First, he doesn't specify *which* emotions can help scientists: curiosity, perplexity, perhaps even anger at the old paradigm? Building on van Fraassen, I want to suggest a crucial role for awe and wonder in scientific practice. As we will see further on, there is a growing empirical literature in support of the importance of this role.[41] Second, van Fraassen doesn't explain how scientists draw on their emotions to change themselves. As I pointed out above, Sartre's theory of emotions is implausibly voluntaristic: it assumes that emotions are under our direct control, when often they are not. However, we can use cognitive technologies to modulate our emotions, so at the very least they are under our indirect control. This also happens in scientific practice, as we will see.

Kant's nebular hypothesis presents a pertinent example of the role of awe for the reception of new and unfamiliar theories. As we saw briefly in chapter 3, Kant formulated a nebular hypothesis for the origin of galaxies.[42] He also proposed that the Milky Way was just one among many galaxies. This could not be established with certainty, because telescopes at the time were too weak. Were faraway nebulae galaxies like the Milky Way? Or were they enormous stars at the fringe of the one galaxy in the universe (ours)? The debate on the size of the universe would continue until the 1920s. Kant argues in favor of multiple galaxies, noting that this hypothesis is "most attractive because of the sublime view it presents of the plan of creation."[43] The faraway nebulae are "systems of many stars, whose distance from us exhibits them as being in so narrow a space that the light, which is imperceptible from each one individually, becomes a uniform pale shimmering with their immeasurable number."[44] He concludes his treatise by discussing the positive sense of awe at the theory that the universe is immeasurably vast, even infinite, as well as old, dynamic, and ever-evolving:

> [W]hen one has filled one's mind with such observations and with the preceding ones, the view of the starry sky on a clear night gives one a kind of pleasure that only noble souls feel. In the universal stillness of nature and the calmness of the senses the immortal spirit's hidden faculty of cognition speaks an ineffable language and provides undeveloped concepts that can certainly be felt but not described.[45]

While the idea of an infinite universe was not new, having been entertained by the Epicureans, Bruno, and Fontenelle, Kant presents a novel vision: he speculates that galaxies could be parts of bigger wholes (what we now know as galaxy clusters), and those parts of even bigger wholes. Much of the appeal of Kant's theory is that it makes us somewhat dizzy with awe, as we zoom out into an ever larger cosmos.

A similar sentiment arises about two centuries later, when, in the final sentence of the first edition of his *Origin of Species*, Darwin expresses awe at his theory of natural selection:

> There is grandeur in this view of life, with its several powers, having been originally breathed into a few forms or into one; and that, whilst this planet has gone cycling on according to the fixed law of gravity, from so simple a beginning endless

> forms most beautiful and most wonderful have been, and are being, evolved.[46]

The need for cognitive accommodation makes you aware there is a lot you do not know. You feel small and part of something bigger. In this way, awe is a self-transcendent emotion because it focuses our attention away from ourselves and toward our environment. It literally helps us to forget ourselves, making our sense of self less salient by focusing on the great thing we feel awe at.[47] Awe is also an epistemic emotion, because it makes us aware of gaps in our knowledge. We can feel overwhelmed looking at the night sky, deeply aware there is so much we don't know about the universe. Likewise, we can look at the dazzling complexity of the natural world, realizing there are so many species, with disparate adaptations and behaviors we know nothing about, even as they are sliding into extinction through our actions.

The philosopher Adam Morton agrees that epistemic emotions play a crucial role in scientific practice.[48] Imagine a scientist who knows the latest research techniques, and who is intelligent and analytical. If she lacks epistemic emotions such as curiosity and awe, she will lack the drive to become a good scientist: she won't be able to change her mind on the basis of evidence, explore new hypotheses, or pay attention to unexpected results. As van Fraassen argues, to change the field or accept radical changes in it, you need to alter your outlook on the world. Awe can do this. It focuses scientists' attention away from themselves and makes them think outside of their usual thought patterns.

Empirical evidence suggests that awe plays a role in the appreciation of science. Many of these studies focus on laypeople rather than working scientists, but they nonetheless provide a tentative glimpse of how awe and science relate. Dispositional awe, the tendency to feel awe, is positively correlated with scientific thinking in non-scientists.[49] Participants with higher dispositional awe have a comparably better grasp of the nature of science; they understand that science is human and fallible, and that it is a collective endeavor. They are also more likely to reject Young Earth creationism. Rather than accepting literalist religious models, they are more receptive to scientific conceptions of the world's origins, which are vast and encompassing. They are also more likely to reject teleological explanations for natural phenomena: for example, they realize that the sun shines because of physical processes, and not with the sole aim of nurturing life on Earth.

When researchers induce awe in participants during their studies, the latter feel more positive toward science. One study showed participants a movie montage of the BBC's *Planet Earth*, a documentary TV series that includes sweeping vistas of waterfalls, canyons, forests, and other scenes of nature. Those in a control condition watched humorous videos of cute animals engaged in capers and antics.[50] People who saw the awe-inspiring videos were more aware of gaps in their knowledge of the natural world than people who watched the funny videos. They were also more likely to choose tickets to a science museum as a reward, rather than tickets to an art museum, compared to the control condition.

A qualitative study by education theorist Megan Cuzzolino probed scientists' conceptions of awe and the role it plays in their work.[51] It consists of semi-structured interviews with professional scientists in various fields of natural science (such as astrophysics, forest ecology, primatology, and neuroscience). For the majority of interviewees, awe was an important motivator for doing science. Awe was associated with gaining knowledge and shifting one's perspective. For example, Ana, a conservation biologist, said that awe

> kind of changes your thinking, or paradigms, or it introduces you to something that you never really thought about. Often to the point of sort of stopping you in your tracks, or making you sort of pause in your thinking.[52]

Another central element of scientific awe is what I have called firstness (and what Cuzzolino calls "seeing with one's own eyes"). Scientists associate awe strongly with first experiences, either witnessing a phenomenon for the first time, or experientially observing something they had predicted theoretically. For example, Ted, an oceanographer who saw waves in the Arctic Ocean that he had predicted theoretically, said,

> Seeing this theory that I've worked on kind of come to fruition in this data, in this place that's very grand, like 3,000 feet of water, and seeing this huge wave that's 600 feet high. That gave me a feeling of awe.[53]

This suggests that eliciting awe would be a good starting point for scientific practice. To get a sense of how this might work, we can return to Heschel's picture of awe and wonder which I outlined in the previous chapter. As we saw, Heschel thought that people are taking the world for granted, thereby losing their ability to experience it with depth and reverence. He does not blame science per se, but rather our attitude to it: we have become complacent when we think that science can solve all our problems, without pausing to think about the marvels that it has in fact revealed to us. Awe and wonder are the antidotes to this complacency. Like Sartre, Heschel held that emotions are a cognitive technology: things we do purposively to change ourselves, and in this way, the world. But unlike Sartre, Heschel did not think that the main transformative effect of emotions was to make an unbearable and conflicted world bearable. Rather, Heschel thought emotions could help us to see the world not in flat, drab, and purely instrumental terms, but as valuable for its own sake, filled with marvels and delights. To gain deep knowledge, of the kind attained by profound scientific insight or, for Heschel, religious wisdom, we should see the world as an end in itself, beautiful and complex. And for that, awe is required.

How is awe evoked? As we saw in the previous chapter, Heschel argued that Jewish rituals are conducive to awe. He conceived of rituals as embodied physical actions that help us to mark certain emotional states in response to the environment. The repetition of ritual practices trains our minds and bodies to respond with awe and wonder to the world around us. By uttering a blessing, you become more attuned to how precious and fleeting are snow, blossoms, meeting a friend, having a nice meal. As we saw, Heschel thinks that rituals push us out of ruts, by edging us into a state of permanent maladjustment, which is conducive to "wonder or radical amazement."[54] This attunes us to see the world in a new light.

While it is easy to see how religious rituals can help to instill awe, it is not so clear how rituals would achieve the same thing in scientific practice. Take scientists who replicate an experiment, who faithfully stick to the minutiae of experimental design. According to philosopher of science Nicholas Shea,

> There may be no good reason for using 10 ml rather than 20 or 5 ml of some solvent, say. This may just be the way it was first done, and since it worked no one has bothered to find out if the quantity could be varied. Indeed, some experiments are so tricky to get right that practitioners show an almost religious adherence to the letter of a known protocol.[55]

This and similar observations of scientists who adhere to ritualistic protocols indicate ritual in science helps scientists feel more secure, or well adjusted. Scientists who do scientific experiments do not want something surprising or awful to happen. However, as Cuzzolino notes, scientists do experience awe in their practice. The majority of scientists she interviewed described scientific practice as an elicitor of awe. This was both when they had a sense of firstness and when they discovered something novel. Sarah, a microbiologist, describes

> a type of awe that comes from making discoveries that no one has known about before. And for a very brief period of time, you are the only person who knows about them and who has ever known about them.[56]

Another road for awe is the scientific sublime, when scientists consider and reflect on the grandeur of the theories they're considering.[57] The scientific sublime may be of crucial importance to help scientists accept things they cannot directly experience, but that are central to scientific theories, such as the genome or plate tectonics. For example, Beth, an epidemiologist, says,

> The first time I had really studied the genome, I remember learning how complex and how perfect it was, and I just remember being floored by it [. . .]. I wanted to tell everybody about it, like, *You guys don't understand how crazy the genome is!* You know, you think it's just a sequence of four letters, randomly, over and over again. But there's so many levels of it, and it's just so perfect.[58]

As Edmund Burke noted, "[t]here are many things of a very affecting nature, which seldom occur in the reality, but the words which represent them often do, and thus they have an opportunity of making a deep impression and of taking root in the mind, whilst the idea of the reality was transient."[59] How can scientists come around to accepting such unobservables, if proof for them can never be definite? Psychologist Benjamin Bradley has argued that Darwin's *Origin of Species* was successful in establishing a new paradigm in part because it relied on a Romantic or Kantian notion of the sublime.[60] While Darwin was not the first to use evolutionary theory to explain how new species come into existence, his work was an unusual combination of scientific rigor and poetic reflection on nature's vastness and complexity. *The Origin of Species* also frequently mentions our lack of knowledge, and our difficulty in imagining the vast timespans under which evolution happens, which are elicitors of awe. For example, Darwin evokes the idea of deep time, by discussing the effects of geological events over vast periods of time:

> Professor Ramsay has published an account of a downthrow in Anglesea of 2,300 feet; and he informs me that he fully believes there is one in Merionethshire of 12,000 feet; yet in these cases there is nothing on the surface to show such prodigious movements; the pile of rocks on the one or other side having been smoothly swept away. The consideration of these facts impresses my mind almost in the same manner as does the vain endeavour to grapple with the idea of eternity.[61]

Awe increases our tolerance for uncertainty and makes us more receptive to the new and unusual ideas which are crucial for paradigm change. We can see this at work in science communicator Mary Somerville's *On the Connexion of the Physical Sciences*, first published in 1834. This book was a hugely popular synthesis of the science of its time. Moreover, it anticipated novel ideas such as the existence of Neptune, due to orbital anomalies, long before the planet was discovered by telescope, and the existence of exoplanets and other not yet detected astronomical matter. Frequently, Somerville appealed to the readers' sense of awe, as here:

> So numerous are the objects which meet our view in the heavens, that we cannot imagine a part of space where some light would not strike the eye; innumerable stars, thousands of double and multiple systems, clusters in one blaze with their tens of thousands of stars, and the nebulæ amazing us by the strangeness of their forms and the incomprehensibility of their nature, till at last, from the limit of our senses, even these thin and airy phantoms vanish in the distance. If such remote bodies shone by reflected light, we should be unconscious of their existence. Each star must then be a sun, and may be presumed to have its system of planets, satellites, and comets, like our own; and, for aught we know, myriads of bodies may be wandering in space unseen by us, of whose nature we can form no idea, and still less of the part they perform in the economy of the universe.[62]

This blending of lyrical poetry and scientific precision exemplifies the scientific sublime. Awe and wonder are not only required for the day-to-day practitioner of science; they are crucial to help reorient scientists' thinking in times of paradigm change. They provide constant emotional motivation for scientists to continue their work, and instill openness to scientific ideas in the public. While precision and rigor are important, the emotional drive of awe and wonder is what matters—it may be, as Heschel speculated, our only path to knowledge and wisdom.[63]

7

Transforming the World through Awe and Wonder

Wondering at the Natural World

In the fantasy novel *A Wizard of Earthsea* (1968) by Ursula K. Le Guin (1929–2018), young Ged (also known by his use-name, Sparrowhawk) is an apprentice to the taciturn wizard Ogion. In the world of Earthsea, a wizard gains power over a thing if he learns its true name in the old dragon speech. Part of Ged's apprenticeship involves learning the true names of things. Rather than seeking prestige and renown for his deeds, Ogion is a recluse, spending most of his time wandering in nature, collecting various herbs. Ged, a quick learner whose temperament is ill-suited to this relaxed pedagogy, wonders what the point of it all is. As they climb the grassy hills of the island Gont, he asks Ogion a question that has been burning at the back of his mind for some time,

> "When will my apprenticeship begin, Sir?"
>
> "It has begun," said Ogion.
>
> There was a silence, as if Ged was keeping back something he had to say. Then he said it: "But I haven't learned anything yet!"
>
> "But you haven't found out what I am teaching," replied the mage [. . .].
>
> "You want to work spells," Ogion said presently, striding along. "You've drawn too much water from that well. Wait. Manhood is patience. Mastery is nine times patience. What is that herb by the path?"
>
> "Strawflower."
>
> "And that?"
>
> "I don't know."
>
> "Fourfoil, they call it." Ogion had halted, the copper-shod foot of his staff near the little weed, so Ged looked closely at the plant, and plucked a dry seedpod from it, and finally asked, since Ogion said nothing more, "What is its use, Master?"
>
> "None I know of."
>
> Ged kept the seedpod a while as they went on, then tossed it away.

> "When you know the fourfoil in all its seasons root and leaf and flower, by sight and scent and seed, then you may learn its true name, knowing its being: which is more than its use. What, after all, is the use of you? or of myself? Is Gont Mountain useful, or the Open Sea?" Ogion went on a half mile or so, and said at last, "To hear, one must be silent."[1]

The tendency to reduce the natural world to things we can use (even exploit) is all-encompassing and difficult to get rid of. Part of the central conflict in *A Wizard of Earthsea* is that Ged is (at this point in the narrative) unable to achieve that shift in perspective. He is solely interested in the power-aspect of magic, and not in its wonder aspect (see chapter 4 for an exploration of this dual aspect of magic). He wants to control, rather than to be in awe. And yet, a central theme in the *Earthsea* cycle is that wonder at the world is necessary for balance, ecological as well as magical. This includes wonder at the brevity, beauty, and limitations of a human lifespan and at our role in a broader history and ecology. Wonder is a virtue that needs cultivation. It will take Ged two more books before he realizes this and comes to fully appreciate his former teacher's wisdom.

Several philosophers have developed the idea that wonder constitutes a kind of virtue. In many of her works, Martha Nussbaum implies an account of wonder and awe as appropriate attitudes we can cultivate in response to living things. There is "something wonderful and worthy of awe" about them.[2] This raises the question: What makes things worthy of wonder and awe? After all, if these are subjective feelings, it would seem you could feel wonder at anything. There's no reason to single out the natural world as especially worthy of wonder.

Jeremy Bendik-Keymer interprets Nussbaum's concept of wonder as *biocentric wonder*.[3] The central thought he teases out of her work is roughly this: in order to flourish, living things have certain interests and requirements, which are particular to their circumstances. What it means for a sea lion to thrive is very different from what it means for an ant or an ash tree. By encouraging a sense of openness to this diversity, wonder makes us more receptive to nonhuman kinds of lives. Our openness helps us see the diversity within the living world, and this, according to Nussbaum, makes us also more attuned to diverse human lives and what they require. The fictional fourfoil is an unspectacular little weed, but looking at it attentively, understanding what contributes to its flourishing, can give us a deeper understanding, not just of that plant, but of the world in general. In this way, wonder gives us a perspective shift. By extension, we might also feel wonder at non-living things, such as crystals, caves, or clouds.

I'll argue in this chapter that wonder can play a crucial role in helping us see nature not as a means, but as valuable in itself. Such a shift is urgently needed, given the existential threat of climate change and the biodiversity crisis. I center this discussion on Rachel Carson's views on wonder as a road to virtue and environmental awareness.

Beyond Self-Help

Awe and wonder are all the rage. Tapping into these emotions would solve a range of problems, including poor mental health and burnout. In *Psychology Today,* we read that a "sense of wonder promotes loving-kindness."[4] In a similar vein, the *New York Times* recommends the practice of awe-walks: you can instantly improve your well-being if you regularly take a walk and "consciously watch for small wonders."[5] And a BBC "Worklife" article informs us that awe can "improve memory, boost creativity and relieve anxious rumination."[6] The underlying idea is that awe and wonder can help us solve problems in our individual lives.

However, those problems—anxiety, rumination, burnout, a sense of alienation and atomization—do not solely originate in us. They are caused by broader societal problems. As philosopher Jonathan Kaplan points out, self-help individualizes solutions to problems that have structural, societal origins.[7] Suggesting awe-walks and nature bathing as a way to relieve stress fails to resolve the fundamental social structure that creates burnout in the first place. Kaplan points out that the phenomenon of self-help originated as part of the women's health movement in the 1970s which emphasized autonomy and mutual aid. Self-help meant seeking out advice from other women on, among other topics, infant-feeding decisions. Today, self-help advice has lost its mutual aid aspect. It has become an industry, with its own bestselling nonfiction genre and gurus.

We sometimes draw on our emotions in ways that do more than merely mitigate our anxieties. Emotions such as anger, love, and exasperation can be deeply transformative. They change who we are, and what our world looks like. In such situations, we are not content with self-soothing and individualizing our collective ills. Consider the widespread phenomenon of climate anxiety or, more broadly, eco-anxiety. This is now also receiving academic attention, due to its negative impact on mental health.[8] Eco-anxiety arises from a sense of loss, particularly of places to which people feel a strong emotional connection, combined with a perceived inability to stop climate change through personal actions. By themselves, such negative emotions can have a stifling effect, because the challenges of catastrophic climate change and the capitalist structures that cause it, combined with lack of political willpower, seem so formidable, leading to the phenomenon of eco-paralysis whereby people become so distressed by the issue that they don't know how to act.[9]

We want to live in a world that is safe and nurturing for everyone, so that everyone can fully experience awe and wonder. We want to preserve such a world for future generations. To do this, some authors have argued, we should nourish our ability to feel awe and wonder at nature *now*, while we are in the maw of ecological collapse. Paleoclimatologist and climate activist Jacquelyn Gill muses,

> When things are hard, I often turn to the natural world for inspiration, strength, and yes, even joy. Sharing this sense of wonder with others makes me feel more connected and grounded, and gives my life meaning. It also reminds me of what I fight for.[10]

She joins the voices of many other scientists who combine their science with activism: awe and wonder at the natural world is, for them, a source of resilience and hope when the outlook is bleak. I want to explore the following question in more detail: How can awe and wonder be sources of hope? And, how would this be different from self-help?

I draw on Rachel Carson's views on awe and wonder, especially as she developed them in her book *The Sense of Wonder* (1965). I argue that Carson sees wonder as a virtue and a self-transformative emotion. To examine how emotions transform us, I'll look at the philosophical literature on self-transformation and at feminist philosophical theories of emotion, in particular by Sara Ahmed and Myisha Cherry. This will bring us closer to an answer to the question of how awe and wonder can help us change. Wonder, like other virtues, changes what we can do by changing our outlook. I'll show that awe and wonder give us two key insights: first, that we are interconnected with the rest of the world; and second, that the things we are in awe of and wonder at are intrinsically valuable.

Rachel Carson's Notion of Awe and Wonder

Rachel Louise Carson (1907–1964) was an American marine biologist and conservationist. During the Great Depression, she wrote radio scripts for the US Bureau of Fisheries, and later became editor-in-chief of all publications for the US Fish and Wildlife Service. In her spare time, she devoted herself to writing books and articles on the natural world for the general public. Notable among these was her trilogy on the sea, written with literary verve and a naturalist's precision: *Under the Sea-Wind* (1941), its prize-winning successor *The Sea around Us* (1951), and *The Edge of the Sea* (1955).

In 1952, following the success of *The Sea around Us*, Carson resigned from her editorial position so she could write full time. Her sea trilogy and other early works are noted for their lyrical quality and the sense of wonder they evoke. Carson's writing is still strongly associated with wonder at nature. However, another emotion features prominently in her later writing: fear. In the late 1950s, Carson became concerned by the widespread and indiscriminate use of pesticides, a concern that would eventually culminate in her book *Silent Spring* (1962). The book warns of the use of chemical insecticides, notably DDT, which was lauded as a miracle solution to insect pests. Her work had an immense influence on the environmental movement, leading to a widespread ban on the use of DDT. It also drew disapproval: critics blamed Carson for a surge of malaria in developing countries.[11]

Fear and wonder may seem emotions that pull us in different directions. Fear entices us to act, wonder to take a step back and contemplate. However, as we saw in chapter 3, there is a domain of aesthetics (and human life more generally) where fear and wonder meet: the sublime. The late Alan G. Gross, a scholar of rhetoric and science communication, read *Silent Spring* and other books by Carson as invoking the scientific sublime: that is, awe and wonder directed at science.[12]

Silent Spring is less lyrical than Carson's other work. But it begins with an unforgettable apocalyptic fable that endures in the collective imagination. It starts, simply, like this:

> There was once a town in the heart of America where all life seemed to live in harmony with its surroundings.

All seemed well until

> a strange blight crept over the area and everything began to change. Some evil spell had settled on the community: mysterious maladies swept the flocks of chickens; the cattle and sheep sickened and died. Everywhere was a shadow of death."[13]

These opening pages don't read like the beginning of a science book, but rather as speculative horror fiction from the 1940s and 1950s—think of Jack Finney's *Body Snatchers* (1954) or John Wyndham's *Midwich Cuckoos* (1957) and their oppressive, eerie atmosphere. Carson continues,

> There was a strange stillness. The birds, for example—where had they gone? Many people spoke of them, puzzled and disturbed. The feeding stations in the backyards were deserted. The few birds seen anywhere were moribund; they trembled violently and could not fly. It was a spring without voices. On the mornings that had once throbbed with the dawn chorus of robins, catbirds, doves, jays, wrens, and scores of other

bird voices there was now no sound; only silence lay over the fields and woods and marsh.[14]

This effective use of rhetoric and the scientific sublime is characteristic of Carson's work throughout. In this case, it is invoking not (as usual) the majesty and force of nature, but its fragility in the face of ill-considered human interventions. As environmental scholar Lisa Sideris notes, Carson's earlier works on the sea instill a sense of wonder that seeks to go beyond the mere learning facts about nature and how to control it, looking rather to re-enchant us.[15] *Silent Spring*, on the other hand, jolts us out of the enchantment of techno-optimism, the overblown rhetoric on pesticides as a magical solution for pest control. Thus, fear and wonder come together.

According to Gross, *Silent Spring* uses sublime imagery of environmental destruction to create a secular Book of Revelation. In the Book of Revelation (the final book of the New Testament), the apocalyptic imagery is intended to strike fear into the hearts of all but the saved. But in the fictional heartland of *Silent Spring*, nobody is saved. Note, however, that Carson was not anti-science. She merely pointed toward an ill-informed use of technology. She proposed, in contrast to this, an enlightened science, "a family of disciplines sensitive to the intricacies of the web of life, the relationships that bind all in a single living and evolving community. This vision demands that our actions be animated by an environmental ethic."[16]

The intertwining of awe, wonder, the sublime, and Carson's moral concerns about the environment are notable features of her philosophy. While she was conceiving *Silent Spring*, she was also planning a book on wonder. She discussed it with her agent, writing that it would be "Heaven to achieve."[17] However, *Silent Spring* took precedence as a writing project, because

Carson felt it addressed a more urgent threat. She was running out of time: she was suffering from breast cancer, which would eventually kill her. Instead of the big, ambitious book on wonder, which would have contained chapters with alluring titles such as "The Sky," "The Woods," "The World of Tiny Things," we are left with a slender volume entitled *The Sense of Wonder*. This is a posthumously published illustrated edition of an essay Carson wrote for the magazine *Women's Home Companion*.[18] In it, she describes the joy she experienced together with her young nephew Roger, as they spent time at the beach along the coast of Maine and other places of natural beauty, and how she helped him to develop a sense of delight for the natural world. The opening paragraph of the book is characteristic of its overall style and tone:

> One stormy autumn night when my nephew Roger was about twenty months old I wrapped him in a blanket and carried him down to the beach in the rainy darkness. Out there, just at the edge of where-we-couldn't-see, big waves were thundering in, dimly seen white shapes that boomed and shouted and threw great handfuls of froth at us. Together we laughed for pure joy—he a baby meeting for the first time the wild tumult of Oceanus, I with the salt of half a lifetime of sea love in me. But I think we felt the same spine-tingling response to the vast, roaring ocean and the wild night around us.[19]

Carson believed that awe and wonder are emotions children naturally possess, though they can be dimmed over time if not properly nurtured or cultivated:

> A child's world is fresh and new and beautiful, full of wonder and excitement. It is our misfortune that for most of us that clear-eyed vision, that true instinct for what is beautiful and

> awe-inspiring, is dimmed and even lost before we reach adulthood.[20]

She also held that awe and wonder not only make us feel good, but that these emotions are also a source of strength in times of difficulty, equal to the vicissitudes of modern life, even death.

> What is the value of preserving and strengthening this sense of awe and wonder, this recognition of something beyond the boundaries of human existence? [. . .] Those who dwell, as scientists or laymen, among the beauties and mysteries of the earth, are never alone or weary of life. Whatever the vexations or concerns of their personal lives, their thoughts can find paths that lead to inner contentment and to renewed excitement in living. Those who contemplate the beauty of the earth find reserves of strength that will endure as long as life lasts.[21]

In Carson's view, awe and wonder are transformative. These emotions help us to see the world differently, and by seeing the world differently, we change too. Wonder is an antidote to our destructive concern with gaining control over nature for our own ends. As she mused in *Lost Woods* (a posthumous collection), this self-destructiveness requires urgent intervention. Wonder is not a single solution to this:

> There is certainly no single remedy for this condition and I am offering no panacea. But it seems reasonable to believe—and I do believe—that the more clearly we can focus our attention on the wonders and realities of the universe about us the less taste we shall have for the destruction of our race. Wonder and humility are wholesome emotions, and they do not exist side by side with a lust for destruction.[22]

However, she does not specify *how* these emotions transform us, or how awe and wonder can be reservoirs of resilience and strength that we can draw upon when the going gets tough. One possible interpretation, proposed by environmental philosopher Kathleen Dean Moore, that I will take here as a guiding idea, is that Carson saw wonder as a kind of virtue.[23] To be a person who wonders is to be a virtuous person who is properly attentive to the intrinsic value of natural beauty. Moore thinks this is because virtue gives us a way to close the distance between "is" and "ought." We feel that "this is wonderful," and therefore, "this must remain." As many philosophers since Hume have pointed out, there is a gap between "is" and "ought." It's not because something is wonderful that we should attempt to preserve it. Virtue helps to close that gap. For a person who possesses the relevant virtue, a state of affairs does come with obligations and courses of actions. For example, if you are patient, you will not rush into things. Virtue attunes you to the environment in a specific way. The virtue of wonder is such an attuner, a "bridge of moral resolve that links the physical world and the moral world [. . . ;] a sense of wonder may well be a moral virtue, perhaps the keystone virtue of an environmental ethic."[24] More specifically, wonder helps us to see the things we wonder at as intrinsically valuable. To become a person who wonders and is in awe of nature is a form of self-transformation. Many religious traditions have fleshed out this intimate connection between awe, wonder, and self-transformation. But we can also explore this naturalistically, as I will show in the remainder of this chapter.

Transformative Awe and Wonder

Stories of transformative awe and wonder abound in religious accounts. Saul of Tarsus, a Roman Jew who persecuted the early Christians, experienced a life-transforming vision of Christ (as recorded in the New Testament in Acts 9 and Galatians 1). He saw a blinding light and heard the voice of the risen Christ who asked him, "Saul, Saul, why are you persecuting me?" This experience left Saul (later Paul) utterly shaken. He was blinded for three days, unable to eat or drink. The vision precipitated his conversion to Christianity. In chapter 11 of the *Bhagavad Gita*, Arjuna converses with his charioteer, who reveals himself as the god Krishna. When he requests that Krishna show himself, Arjuna witnesses a dazzling display of Krishna as Lord of the Universe, "an entire universe moving and unmoving all at once in my body," with the intensity of a thousand suns rising all at once. In response, Arjuna "was so amazed that his hair was standing on end."[25] Thus, he overcomes his qualms at fighting his relatives in the decisive battle for power over the kingdom.

In their suddenness and intensity, the spiritual-transformative stories of Paul and Arjuna fit well into an influential account of transformative experience, as developed by the philosopher L. A. Paul: a transformative experience is an event that changes a person in both who they are and what they know.[26] One of her prime examples is giving birth to and raising a child (though the process can also describe adopting one). Giving birth or adopting a child is a process you go into not knowing how it will be for you, and it changes you in one fell swoop. But as we saw in chapter 5, religious transformations can also be gradual, as one habituates oneself to new religious practices. Some transformative experiences are ones we deliberately choose: for example, many people today can decide when they will try to have children. The philosopher Richard Pettigrew calls this phenomenon "choosing for changing selves," and he notes that the change doesn't always happen all at once.[27] But not all transformative experiences are by choice. Havi Carel and Ian Kidd argue that the philosophical literature on transformative experiences has put too much emphasis on rational deliberation and free choice, neglecting the fact that many of our transformative experiences are unchosen—such as illness, disability, domestic violence, or unemployment.[28] Even in situations where we can choose, we often do so under imperfect conditions. As Carel and Kidd object, "some people cannot engage in a rational deliberative procedure, if subjection to oppression, violence, and neglect has left them overwhelmed, traumatised, or in some other way cognitively and epistemically compromised."[29] Many philosophers, notably Aristotle, Martha Nussbaum, and Alasdair MacIntyre, have argued that our well-being and flourishing depend on luck and circumstance. We are vulnerable to afflictions or benefit from good fortunes that are largely beyond our control. Human lives are a combination of deterministic and stochastic processes.

If our rationality is compromised by imperfect conditions, how can we ever rationally "choose for changing selves"? This remains an unresolved question in the philosophical literature. As we have seen, Carson, Gill, and other authors hold that we can draw on awe and wonder, and choose to transform ourselves. This can help us become more resilient and more attentive to our environment. But how do emotions help us do this, and how is changing selves different from individualized self-help? A potential answer lies in feminist philosophy, notably Black feminism, which has explored in depth how we can be agents who can choose for changing selves, even under very limiting conditions, including structural oppression.

Wonder as Firstness, Emotions as Catalysts for Change

Feminist philosopher Sara Ahmed connects wonder to feminism. Pushing back against the portrayal of feminism as an overtly gloomy philosophy born of solely negative emotions such as rage, anger, or pain, she argues that her (and other people's) impulse to feminism is also born of wonder.[30] Drawing on Descartes's notion of wonder as the first passion, she premises wonder on firstness: that is, encountering an object as if we are seeing it for the first time. In Ahmed's view, to wonder is to assume an as-if stance, a stance whereby we cease to take an object we wonder at for granted. In this way "wonder works to transform the ordinary, which is already recognised, into the extraordinary."[31] Seeing something as if we see it for the first time does not require that we erase history. Rather, it "allows us to see the surfaces of the world as made, and as such wonder opens up rather than suspends historicity."[32]

Ahmed situates her work within the tradition of wonder as a philosophical emotion par excellence, which allows us to see the old and the taken-for-granted with new eyes. As such, her conception of wonder is not child-like, because the wonder we feel doesn't suspend our background knowledge. Rather, it actively uses that background knowledge—for instance, about power and gender relations, and their history—to reconsider our current situation. Looking at an antique postcard of a city, for example, can generate a sense of wonder at the current layout of the place and things we take for granted about it, such as the infrastructure for cars and lack of local stores. Looking at the postcard, you ask yourself, "Did things have to turn out this way?" This wonder not only transforms how we see the world; it also transforms the person who wonders.

Black feminist authors such as Audre Lorde, bell hooks, and most recently Myisha Cherry, have examined how emotions can be both personally and politically transformative. Much of their work on emotions and politics focuses on anger. Anger has a bad rap in many philosophical traditions, ranging from Buddhism to Stoicism. Many philosophers regard it as unproductive, irrational, and an obstacle to more positive emotions.

Owen Flanagan, a contemporary anger-skeptic, argues that anger cannot be moderated and hence tends to overshoot.[33] Even if our anger is righteous, its effects are negative. It fires at the wrong targets; it cannot be tempered or rightly dosed. We can see a slightly less negative view of anger in Nussbaum, who thinks that anger can be useful as a transitional state: justice can only happen once anger has made room for love and generosity.[34]

Against these critics of anger, Cherry makes the case for transformative anger.[35] Building on and further developing an account by Lorde, she argues that anger in itself can be productive. For Lorde, feelings can be a source of knowledge, particularly when we are in a situation where we have limited other information, such as lack of a community of peers or formal sources.[36] Lorde struggled to understand how racism negatively affected her. She also tried to make sense of her lesbian orientation. In the absence of literature or of peers, she found it useful to turn to the individual feelings that governed her everyday life.[37] If injustices and racial prejudice make you angry, then that anger can be an important signal of something that is deeply wrong, even if society at large does not see the structures that give rise to your sense of anger as problematic. Feelings *can* be a source of knowledge, particularly if we have few other resources to draw on. This is not to say emotions are a reliable source of knowledge, or that we should place them above the facts that are available to us. Rather, they ought not to be dismissed out of hand as a potential source of knowledge and, in the absence of other information, they can be valuable. There are thus situations in which we can trust our anger, wonder, or hope.

For Cherry, transformative anger aims for change.[38] It motivates us to try to alter the way society views the world. Anger challenges racist beliefs, expectations, policies, and behaviors. The person experiencing rage "would aim to tackle racism head-on by seeking to change the world, so that racism is no more." Cherry doesn't claim that anger always has positive results, or that it cannot go wrong, or that it is the only apt emotion to feel in response to racial injustices. But she argues that it is a fitting emotion in the face of racism. Cherry and Ahmed present a striking contrast to the idea of emotions as individualized self-soothing and self-help. Individualized self-help tells us to cultivate certain emotions and dispositions, such as hope and awe, as ways to make us individually more resilient in situations that are the result of structural injustices. But self-help says nothing about tackling those injustices. By contrast, Black feminism says that emotions can also be used to change the world, to tackle the structures that actively harm and sometimes seek deliberately to destroy us. Given the emphasis on anger, we might think that this is specific to anger and cannot be generalized to other emotions. But, as Ahmed points out, wonder too can be transformative.[39] The question then becomes how awe and wonder can help us to achieve self-transformation, and in this way, world-transformation.

Awe and Wonder as Virtues

We might be motivated to counter climate change because it is ultimately economically beneficial to do so. Climate change is bad because wildfires, displacement of people, and loss of agricultural yields harm the economy. We even measure the worth of human lives in terms of money, and illness in terms of GDP loss. Training videos at work tell us harassment is bad because it lowers productivity. Heschel hypothesized that this focus on material wealth is characteristic of modern life, caused in part by our lack of awe and wonder for the world we live in.[40] Awe and wonder, however, as non-utilitarian emotions, help us to see things not as means to economic or other ends, but as valuable in themselves. Carson argued that we need to cultivate our sense of wonder, otherwise it fades, just like other virtuous dispositions such as resilience need to be cultivated.[41] Once we have trained our ability to wonder, our sense of what is possible shifts. We no longer have to see things in terms of their usefulness, or their monetary value. We can see them as richer, fuller, complex, and autonomous.

We can interpret Carson's views on wonder in virtue ethical terms. According to virtue ethicists such as Philippa Foot (1920–2010) and Alasdair MacIntyre, virtues occupy a central place in our ethical lives. Virtues are excellent character traits that shape who we are. Examples include patience, wisdom, honesty, courage, and humility. They run deeper than mere habits, such as getting up early in the morning, or drinking a lot of coffee. Rather, virtues shape our habits, and are in turn shaped by our habits. Because they so thoroughly form us, virtues allow us to admit moral considerations into the constellation of careful thoughts we entertain when we decide on a course of action. Imagine a state official who is tempted by a bribe. If she is honest, then the benefits of the bribe won't enter into her moral considerations. Her main concern is not, "Will I be caught?" A virtuous person would not even think as far as wondering if she would be caught. We might say, to use a phrase of John McDowell's, that virtues *silence* competing considerations, rather than outweighing them.[42]

This virtue ethical reading brings us closer to a possible explanation of how wonder helps us to see things we wonder at as intrinsically valuable. As virtue ethicist Denise Vigani argues, we tend to think of virtue as foreclosing possibilities.[43] For example, it would not enter an honest person's mind to take a bribe, nor would it enter a humble person's mind to brag.

However, virtues can also open up new possibilities. They enable people to see potential paths of action that aren't options to those who don't share the relevant virtue. Keeping Descartes in mind, when you wonder at something, you are not yet taking an evaluative stance, in terms of whether the object you wonder at would harm or help you. You simply meet the object or event that is unfamiliar to you on its own terms. Continued cultivation of wonder as a virtue requires that we treat even things we are familiar with as new, at least on occasion. Why might this be? For one thing, we know a lot less about the natural world than we think we do. This is the case not only for laypeople, but also for experts. Wondering at old questions, such as why zebras have stripes, or why butterflies are colorful, can yield new and intriguing answers. Moreover, we can discover new aspects to things we think we are familiar with by keeping our sense of wonder alive. Wonder can alert us to beautiful and alluring parts of our world we have become desensitized to, such as birdsong in the morning. Finally, because they encourage self-reflection, awe and wonder also prompt us to see the broader relationships between ourselves and the things we wonder at. As we saw in chapter 3, because awe is associated with vastness, it gives rise to a feeling of being part of a big and interconnected cosmos. Thus, awe and wonder can give rise to a sense of being interconnected not only with our fellow human beings, but also with nature and even the universe at large.[44]

We saw at the beginning of this chapter how we can cultivate our sense of wonder at nature by valuing the natural world for its own sake. Nature is worth wondering at, and by engaging earnestly with its diversity of life forms, we can become more aware of their intrinsic worth. We have tools to help us develop this sense of wonder. Although it is possible to wonder at nature with little, if any, background knowledge, in the way a young child does, we can support our sense of wonder through cultural means. For example, the collective celebration of blossom viewing (*hanami*) in Japan gives people a culturally structured occasion to marvel at the evanescent beauty of cherry blossoms. Likewise, the first snow in South Korea (*cheotnun*) is a moment of celebration. Both romantic and existential significance is attached to the viewing of the very first snowflakes on a given year. People stop for a moment, come out to witness the event, and kiss their lovers. Festivals of light, such as Dev Deepavali on the Ganges or Yi Peng in Thailand, with lanterns that float up into the sky, are celebrated throughout the world. Whale viewings, bat walks, and looking for fireflies are also activities people undertake together to inspire a sense of awe and wonder in their lives. So are, by extension, sports events, fireworks displays, air shows, or public science events such as Science Week.

These collective events are mutually supportive of awe and wonder. They are nurtured by our sense of wonder and help to rekindle that sense in the face of many countervailing forces. Moreover, by making such cognitive technologies part and parcel of our cooperative ventures, they help us cultivate the virtue of wonder collectively. If we want to have more room for awe and wonder in our lives, we need more cognitive technologies that make this possible for us as interconnected societies.

8

Epilogue

RECLAIMING OUR SENSE OF WONDER

IN JANUARY 2022, I was supposed to give my first in-person talk after the unrelenting nearly two-year slog of working in higher education during a pandemic. I looked forward to meeting the congregation of the Ethical Society of Saint Louis, a secular humanist community loosely modeled on a church.

Then the highly contagious SARS-CoV-2 Omicron variant hit, causing a fresh tsunami of infections, and my talk went virtual.

Surveying the mosaic of small moving portraits on a Zoom screen (each one a microcosm), I spoke about awe and wonder to this live audience, testing some of the materials that ended up in the book you are reading now. One of the congregants, a middle-aged woman, sighed, "I sure look forward to reading this book. I miss a spark of wonder in my life. I haven't experienced awe in ages either." An older man concurred: travel afforded so many opportunities for wonder, but trips or touring had not been part of his life of late. Travel requires leisure time, money, health, and freedom from the responsibility to care for elderly or young dependents. Perhaps, like health, feeling secure, and material comfort, our ability to experience awe and wonder depends on externalities beyond our control. Perhaps they are yet another form of privilege for those lucky enough to travel to the Grand Canyon in the US, Victoria Falls in Zambia and Zimbabwe, the Golden Bridge in Vietnam, or other wonders of the world.

However, awe and wonder are also modes of perception. We can choose to see things with firstness, and for that, we do not need to travel anywhere. You can watch the sun pour through a stained-glass window in the afternoon, dust motes falling onto a warm hardwood floor. You can observe people as they talk together quietly in a café, say their goodbyes at a train station, or rush to catch the bus, allowing you glimpses of a bigger picture of lives intertwined. These delicate social dances are atoms briefly coalescing in time, creating our everyday situations, our mundane concerns. Any connection to nature, even in a bland suburban environment, such as a hardy dandelion growing from between paving stones, affords opportunities for wonder.

You can radically question the nature of reality and yourself, as René Descartes reported in his *Meditations* (1641). Having taught philosophy for many years (including that particular book), I can attest that philosophical speculations—both for novices and experts—are, or can become again, a source of wonder. We can also find solace and wonder in literary fiction and visual art, not purely as a means to escape, but as a way to expand our sense of the possible and to question our reality. This kind of wonder resists resolutions or a clear teleology. It propels us to query the everydayness of our existence, and pushes us to change.

Allowing wonder into one's life is antithetical to despair. Walker Percy's novel *The Moviegoer* (1961) tells of a spiritual quest, which the main character Jack "Binx" Bolling describes as "the search":

> "What is the nature of the search?" you ask.
>
> Really it is very simple; at least for a fellow like me. So simple that it is easily overlooked.
>
> The search is what anyone would undertake if he were not sunk in the everydayness of his own life. This morning, for example, I felt as if I had come to myself on a strange island.[1]

The search occurs to him at intervals—on the bus, in the movie theater, whenever he's not overwhelmed by the drudgery of day-to-day life. He seeks it out; he cannot let go of it: "To become aware of the possibility of the search is to be onto something. Not to be onto something is to be in despair."[2]

Why has the search, this wonder-quest, become so hard? I don't mean hard as in difficult, but as in hard to conceive. To undertake the search requires that time feel ample, stretchy, and flexible, with space for at least some undirected leisure—not in the service of some productivity goal, but truly ours. A number of philosophers, including Heidegger and Heschel, have tried to diagnose what went wrong with wonder and why we feel less of it today. It is common to see the decline of wonder as a direct result of modernity—modern technology and science in particular having caused us to lose our sense of magic. However, as Jason Josephson Storm points out (and as we have seen throughout this book), modernity offers new opportunities for awe and wonder, too.[3] Notably, science gives us insight into how the world is a far more wondrous place than we thought possible. I agree with Storm that the sciences offer us lots of opportunities for awe and wonder. Nonetheless, we have become increasingly alienated from the natural world, a major source of awe and wonder. For instance, in most of the world we are no longer able to witness the starry night sky that inspired so much admiration in the minds of Fontenelle and Kant: A recent report estimates that more than eighty percent of the world population and more than ninety-nine percent of the US and European populations live under light-polluted skies.[4] The Milky Way is no longer visible to sixty percent of Europeans and nearly eighty percent of North Americans.

Also contributing to our loss of awe and wonder is the fact that we are pushed to use *ourselves* for productive ends, as fodder for the economy, our employers, and their shareholders. Even our future selves urge us to work hard to secure our future careers or our retirement, or our children's college funds. Wonder requires attention, and a lot of that is captured by others, such as social media companies, for *their* own ends. As James Williams argues in *Stand Out of Our Light* (2018), contemporary mass media actively sabotage our efforts and obscure our goals in terms of personal connection and living a truthful life. Williams likens tech giants to a faulty GPS that is "adversarial against you."[5] Not only does it not bring you to the place you want to reach; it actively leads you *away* from your intended destination. A sense of despair and powerlessness sucks the air out of us, shrinking that broader philosophical space we are so desperately in need of. We end up bitter, polarized, fragmented.

The key to fighting this hostile environment is to resist the grabs for our attention and to retake control of our headspace, so that we can again have undirected leisure time that would allow us to re-experience awe and wonder. These emotions are not some sort of augmented reality wherein the world is beautified by a sense of unfamiliarity. Rather, they allow us to question the structure of our reality. Take our social conventions. We are born into them, and we shape them a bit either by adhering to them or by resisting them. For example, in Western societies, there remains an expectation of marriage. If you marry, you go with the social conventions; if you do not, you go against them. If many people resist them, social conventions can change, however. In many European countries marriage is no longer the social ideal it once was. Although they are real, social norms are more moldable than our physical reality, such as gravity. As Olúfẹ́mi Táíwò points out, it is beneficial—sometimes necessary—to wonder at our social conventions.[6] Wonder shapes what we think is possible, or helps us to question what we think is immutable. As a European who recently moved to the US, I keep on wondering about the differences in social conventions: for instance, the fact that in the US most women still take their husband's surname.

In 2014, when Ursula Le Guin received the National Book Foundation Medal for Distinguished Contribution to American Letters honoring her long career of writing speculative fiction, she thanked the award committee for giving credit to "realists of a larger reality": the poets, writers of fantasy and science fiction, and visionaries. The wonder they offer through their speculations, she said, may help us realize that "any human power can be resisted and changed by human beings."[7] This sort of wonder doesn't arise from a lack of background knowledge. It is defiance in the face of the current state of affairs, *in spite of* our background knowledge.

Wonder involves looking at the world with a sense of firstness. Its immediacy and suddenness force us right into the moment, to "consider with attention the objects that seem to it unusual and extraordinary."[8] It incites us to learn by challenging our ways of thinking and how we believe the world to be. It is hard to maintain awe and wonder in the face of dreadful news cycles and the drudgery of our lives, which are ever more channeled into narrow, predictable paths by large corporations, governments, and social conventions.

Though many of us feel alienated from what gives us a sense of wonder, it is important to reclaim that sense. This doesn't happen in one fell swoop. We can train ourselves to become more wonder-prone and to cultivate an ethical sensibility to the things we wonder at. Philosophy as a practice and an orientation to life can help with this. It is not a denial of the realities of life, nor does it mean a stolid acceptance of whatever life throws at us (as the common usage of the adjective "philosophical" suggests). Rather, as Merleau-Ponty characterized it, philosophical reflection is

> wonder in the face of the world [. . . ;] it steps back to watch the forms of transcendence fly up like sparks from a fire; it slackens the intentional threads which attach us to the world and thus brings them to our notice. It alone is consciousness of the world because it reveals that world as strange and paradoxical.[9]

The world *is* strange and paradoxical, but we're mired in everydayness and so we often forget that. Philosophy is a powerful cognitive technology that reminds us of this strangeness. By giving us the tools to keep our awe and wonder alive, it allows us the mental space to consider possibilities. In this way, we are offered the tantalizing possibility of making human culture again something that responds to *our* needs, not something to feed the abstract beast of the economy. Awe and wonder can then become catalysts that help us to reclaim what makes life worth living, or, as William James put it, "to make the notion of mere existence tolerable."[10]

ACKNOWLEDGMENTS

This book could not have been written without the help and support of many people. Thank you to my editor Rob Tempio and his editorial assistant Chloe Coy at Princeton University Press. I am grateful to Rob for his encouragement and support throughout, as well as his suggestion to write this book for a wide audience. Also thank you to Francis Eaves, copy editor for Princeton University Press. I have drawn on the expertise of many people who have read parts or the whole of the manuscript at various stages of its development, including Frederick Choo, Tom Cochrane, Alice Harberd, Daniel Helman, Heather Kresge, Jeremy Pober, Donovan Schaefer, John Teehan, Marilyn Vogel, Justin White, Jennifer Whyte, Jack Williams, Dean Zimmerman, and Perry Zurn, and my research assistants Isabel Cortens and Katie Rackers. I am grateful for having been able to discuss some of the practical arts mentioned in this book with magicians Larry Hass and Matt Pritchard, and wonder-cabinet maker Hester Loeff.

I am also grateful to organizers and audiences at several events where I could present some of the ideas in this book. These include the Personality and Social Psychology Annual Convention in San Francisco, the workshop on religious epistemology at Rutgers University, the University of Georgia, the Ethical Society of St Louis, and Cogweirdo, the Halloween edition of CogTweeto's online workshops. Thank you for hosting me and for your valuable feedback.

Most of all, I am indebted to my family for putting up with over two years of intensive writing, some of which was done under the difficult circumstances of a pandemic. I am grateful to my children Aliénor and Gabriel. My daughter also read an early draft of this book with an eye of making it accessible to a beginning-college student audience. My husband Johan De Smedt offered valuable critique on the first full draft.

NOTES

Chapter 1

1. Neil deGrasse Tyson, https://twitter.com/neiltyson/status/1526034149546639361, May 16, 2022 (retrieved June 24, 2023).

2. De Smedt and De Cruz, "The role of material culture."

3. NASA, "NASA's Webb delivers deepest infrared image of universe yet."

4. Technically, the expansion of the universe doesn't have a speed, but we can still talk about how fast galaxies far away from us seem to be receding. Extrapolating to sufficiently large distances implies a recession velocity faster than light, which in practice means that light from those galaxies doesn't reach us. I thank Sean Carroll for clarifying this.

5. A substantial philosophical literature is concerned with how emotions and feelings might differ from each other, see, for example, Arango-Muñoz and Michaelian, "Epistemic feelings, epistemic emotions." I'll later make some finer-grained distinctions, but here I'll treat emotions and feelings as roughly synonymous.

6. Morton, "Epistemic emotions."

7. Stellar et al., "Self-transcendent emotions and their social functions."

8. For a discussion on the value of philosophy, see Van Norden, *Taking Back Philosophy*, 110–11.

9. Brown, *Human Universals*.

10. I specify "in material terms" because the scarcity narrative emphasizes this. However, there are other frameworks according to which peoples with few material resources are not worse off compared to industrialized Westerners, as well-being can be achieved with minimal material means, and many of the cultural resources that help increase it are not material.

11. Dennett, *Breaking the Spell*.

12. Sperber, *Explaining Culture*.

13. For religion: Asma, *Why We Need Religion*; Purzycki and Sosis, *Religion Evolving*; for technology: Richerson and Boyd, *Not by Genes Alone*; about culture in general: Henrich, *The Secret of Our Success*; Heyes, *Cognitive Gadgets*.

14. White, *The Evolution of Culture*, 9. Many older sources use the singular "man" and variations thereon to denote humankind or the whole of humanity. I use more inclusive language, but not when I directly quote these older sources.

15. White, *The Evolution of Culture*, 17.

16. James, "Remarks on Spencer's definition of mind."

17. Spencer's *Principles of Psychology* was published in 1855, four years before Darwin's *On the Origin of Species*.

18. James, "Remarks on Spencer's definition of mind," 2.

19. Ibid., 7.

20. Ibid.

21. Ibid., 8.

22. Brown, *Descartes and the Passionate Mind*.

23. Greenberg, "Descartes on the passions."

24. Descartes, "Passions of the soul," 26, CSM 1:338.

25. Ibid., 212, CSM 1:404.

26. Hadot, *Philosophy as a Way of Life*, 102.

27. Descartes, "Passions of the soul," 70, CSM 1:353.

28. Frazer, *The Golden Bough*.

29. See also my edited volume, De Cruz, *Philosophy Illustrated*.

30. Berger, *The Art of Philosophy*.

Chapter 2

1. André, *La Vie de R .P. Malebranche*, 12 (my translation).

2. Hume, *An Enquiry concerning Human Understanding*, § 4.

3. *Zhuangzi*, bk 17, 188.

4. Most, "Philosophy begins in wonder."

5. Plato, *"Theaetetus" and "Sophist"*, c10, d1, d5, 19.

6. Most, "Philosophy begins in wonder."

7. Aristotle, *Metaphysics*, A.2 982b11–20.

8. Bynum, "Wonder."

9. Prinz, "How wonder works."

10. See Hooke, *Micrographia*, preface (page unnumbered). Modern readers can enjoy a digitized version of *Micrographia*, available via the Royal Society website at https://royalsociety.org/blog/2020/07/micrographia-online/ (accessed June 26, 2023)

11. Hooke, *Micrographia*, observation LIII, 210.

12. Ibid., observation II, 5.

13. Ibid, preface.

14. Ibid.

15. Fontenelle, *Conversations on the Plurality of Worlds.*

16. The modern psychological novel was gaining popularity during this time. Commercially successful novels of this period include *La Princesse de Montpensier* (1662) and *La Princesse de Clèves* (1678), both written by Madame de La Fayette.

17. Fontenelle, *Conversations on the Plurality of Worlds,* 10.

18. Ibid, 11.

19. Fontenelle was an enthusiastic proponent of Descartes's vortex theory, explicated in *Le Monde* (*The World*: see Descartes, "The World, or Treatise on Light"), which holds that the universe is filled with circling bands of material particles, in which the planetary orbits and other celestial motions are embedded.

20. Fontenelle, *Conversations on the Plurality of Worlds,* 63.

21. Ibid.

22. Pascal, *Pensées,* S 230/L 199.

23. Ibid., 58.

24. Ibid., 59.

25. Ibid.

26. Classic experiments such as the double slit experiment (in which single particles, fired through two slits, behave in a wave-like pattern that interferes with itself even though the particles are fired consecutively) have puzzled physicists for over a century, and have led them to propose radical views of reality, such as the hypothesis that there are many worlds, where all possible outcomes of quantum measurements are physically realized.

27. Hammond, "Pascal's *Pensées* and the art of persuasion."

28. Pascal, *Pensées,* 59 (translator's italic insertion).

29. Brown, *Descartes and the Passionate Mind.*

30. Just as our current terminology for feelings is messy (with such terms as "emotions," "affects," "feelings," and "moods" sometimes used interchangeably, at other times more clearly distinguished, as we'll see in the next chapter), early modern terminology was also diverse. Some authors used "passions," others "sentiments," rarely also "emotions." These terms do not overlap entirely with our use of "emotions" and "feelings," but there is enough similarity to see the early modern philosophical study of the passions as a precursor to our contemporary work on emotions.

31. Descartes, "Passions of the soul," 69, CSM 1:353.

32. Ibid., 53, CSM I, 350.

33. Zurn, "Wonder and *écriture*," 116.

34. Descartes, "Passions of the soul," 70, CSM 1:353.

35. Ibid., 70, CSM 1:353.

36. Ibid., 71, CSM 1:353.

37. Ibid.

38. Greenberg, "Descartes on the passions."

39. Descartes, "Passions of the soul," 75, CSM 1:354.

40. Ibid., 75, CSM I:355.

41. Spinoza, "Short treatise on God, man, and his well-being," KV II 3, G1/57.

42. Spinoza, "Ethics demonstrated in geometric order."

43. Brassfield, "Never let the passions be your guide."

44. Descartes, "Passions of the soul," 50, CSM 1:348.

45. Ibid., 76, CSM 1:355.

46. Zurn, "Wonder and *écriture*."

47. Descartes, "The World, or Treatise on light," CSM 1:97.

48. Descartes, "Passions of the soul," 147, CSM 1:381.

49. Brown, *Descartes and the Passionate Mind*, 150.

50. Smith, "The history of astronomy," § 2, 12.

51. One delightful example is Jacques Gallot's *Chaconne la comète*, which musically imitates the splendor of the comet on a Baroque lute.

52. Smith, "The history of astronomy," 3.

53. Ibid.

54. Ibid., § 2, 21.

55. Schliesser, *Adam Smith*, 77.

56. Peirce, "The fixation of belief."

57. Hume, "The natural history of religion."

58. Smith, "The history of astronomy," § 3, 36.

59. Ibid., § 2, 16.

60. Ibid., § 2, 17.

61. Ibid., § 4, 44.

62. Kim, "Adam Smith's *History of Astronomy* and view of science."

63. Smith, "The history of astronomy," § 2, 27.

64. Schliesser, "Wonder in the face of scientific revolutions."

65. Kuhn, *The Structure of Scientific Revolutions*.

66. Smith, "The history of astronomy," § 2: 21–22.

Chapter 3

1. See, e.g., Deonna and Scherer, "The case of the disappearing intentional object."

2. James, "What is an emotion?"

3. For example, Cochrane, *The Emotional Mind*.

4. For example, Seth, *Being You*; Godfrey-Smith, *Metazoa*.

5. Vivaldo et al., "The network of plants volatile organic components."

6. Godfrey-Smith, *Metazoa*, 59.

7. Frijda, *The Emotions*, 7.

8. Cochrane, *The Emotional Mind*.

9. Koelsch et al., "The quartet theory of human emotions."

10. Lewontin, "The organism as the subject and object of evolution."

11. Ekman, "Basic emotions," 46 (italics in original).

12. Ekman, Sorenson, and Friesen, "Pan-cultural elements in facial displays of emotion."

13. Keltner et al., "Emotional expression."

14. Nesse, "Evolutionary explanations of emotions."

15. Keltner and Haidt, "Social functions of emotions."

16. See Tracy and Randles, "Four models of basic emotions," for a review.

17. Keltner et al., "Emotional expression."

18. Barrett, "Are emotions natural kinds?"

19. Russell, "Culture and the categorization of emotions."

20. See, e.g., the work by Tim Lomas on words relating to happiness and well-being in a wide range of languages: Lomas, "Towards a positive cross-cultural lexicography."

21. Girten, "'Sublime luxuries' of the Gothic edifice."

22. Kirkham and Letheby, "Psychedelics and environmental virtues."

23. Rietveld, "Situated normativity."

24. Krueger, "Affordances and the musically extended mind."

25. Oliver, "Tender affective states."

26. Smail, *On Deep History and the Brain.*

27. Clark and Chalmers, "The extended mind."

28. Hutchins, "The cultural ecosystem of human cognition."

29. De Smedt and De Cruz, "The role of material culture in human time representation."

30. Gladwin, *East is a Big Bird.*

31. Ibid., 2.

32. Ibid., 131.

33. Griffiths and Scarantino, "Emotions in the wild."

34. Stephan, Walter, and Wilutzky, "Emotions beyond brain and body."

35. Heyes, *Cognitive Gadgets.*

36. Masuda et al., "Placing the face in context."

37. Bai et al., "Awe, the diminished self, and collective engagement."

38. See Pober, "What emotions really are," for a similar view.

39. Pinker, *How the Mind Works*, 514–25.

40. De Smedt and De Cruz, "Toward an integrative approach."

41. Keltner and Haidt, "Approaching awe."

42. Shiota, Keltner, and Mossman, "The nature of awe"; Piff et al., "Awe, the small self, and prosocial behavior."

43. Danvers, O'Neil, and Shiota, "The mind of the 'happy warrior.'"

44. Bai et al., "Awe, the diminished self, and collective engagement."

45. Keltner, *Awe.*

46. Bai et al., "Awe, the diminished self, and collective engagement."

47. Piff et al., "Awe, the small self, and prosocial behavior."

48. Chen and Mongrain, "Awe and the interconnected self."

49. Tversky and Kahneman, "Judgment under uncertainty."

50. Blanchette and Richards, "The influence of affect on higher level cognition."

51. Clore and Huntsinger, "How emotions inform judgment."

52. Gordon et al., "The dark side of the sublime."

53. Danvers and Shiota, "Going off script"; Griskevicius, Shiota, and Neufeld, "Influence of different positive emotions on persuasion processing."

54. Cochrane, "The emotional experience of the sublime."

55. Burke, *A Philosophical Enquiry.*

56. Clewis, "Why the sublime is aesthetic awe."

57. Kant, "Observations on the feeling of the beautiful and sublime."

58. Cited in Zuckert, "Awe or envy."

59. Cochrane, "The emotional experience of the sublime."

60. Kant, *Critique of Practical Reason,* 162: 203 (italics in original).

61. Kant, "Universal natural history," 1:256, 222.

62. Ibid., 1:314, 266.

63. Kant, *Critique of Practical Reason,* 162: 203.

64. Ibid. (italics in original).

65. Ibid., 162: 20 (italics in original).

66. Algoe and Haidt, "Witnessing excellence in action"; Thomson and Siegel, "Elevation."

67. Keltner and Haidt, "Approaching awe"; Shiota, Keltner, and Mossman, "The nature of awe."

68. Keltner et al., "Emotional expression."

69. Potts, *Humanity's Descent.*

70. Keltner and Piff, "Self-transcendent awe," 161.

71. Frijda, *The Emotions,* 18.

72. Darbor et al., "Experiencing versus contemplating."

73. Shiota, "Awe, wonder, and the human mind," 86.

Chapter 4

1. Agrippa, *Three Books of Occult Philosophy,* 18.

2. This trick is "Silverfish," devised by the magician Teller. It is his original take on the Miser's Dream, a magic routine in which a magician produces coins out of thin air and drops them into a receptacle.

3. See, e.g., Copenhaver, *Magic in Western Culture*.

4. Hass, "Life magic and staged magic," 14.

5. Goto-Jones, *Conjuring Asia*, 33–34.

6. Sanderson, *The Hero of Ages*, 29.

7. Sanderson, "Sanderson's First Law." Sanderson's fellow panelists are not named.

8. Throughout the *Earthsea* books, the hard aspect of magic is questioned. One of the major character arcs in the cycle, about the wizard Ged, is the repudiation of hard magic in favor of soft magic as practiced by the elusive dragons. We'll return to this in chapter 7.

9. Levy and Mendlesohn, *Children's Fantasy Literature*.

10. Teller, "What Is Magic?".

11. Lamont, "A particular kind of wonder."

12. Rolfe, "Theatrical magic and the agency to enchant the world."

13. Boyer, *Religion Explained*.

14. Porubanova et al., "Memory for expectation-violation concepts."

15. In the early days of psychology, there was some attention given to magicians' skills. Much of this was devoted to their manual dexterity and speed. Joseph Jastrow, for example, tested the manual dexterity and memory of two prestidigitators (illusionists who work through sleight of hand) in a range of tasks, and found (to his surprise) that there were only small differences between magicians and non-magicians. Both illusionists performed within the range of what other, non-magician, participants could do: Jastrow, "Psychological notes upon sleight-of-hand experts."

16. Cavanagh, "The artist as neuroscientist."

17. Rensink and Kuhn, "A framework for using magic."

18. Seneca, "On sophistical argumentation," 295.

19. Pailhès and Kuhn, "Influencing choices with conversational primes"; Kuhn, Pailhès, and Lan, "Forcing you to experience wonder."

20. Smith, *History of Astronomy*, § 1, 3.

21. Ibid., § 2, 21.

22. Parris et al., "Imaging the impossible."

23. Garcia-Pelegrin et al., "Exploring the perceptual inabilities of Eurasian Jays."

24. Legare and Souza, "Evaluating ritual efficacy."

25. Alves, Rosa, and Santana, "The role of animal-derived remedies."

26. Legare and Nielsen, "Ritual explained."

27. Malinowski, *Magic, Science, and Religion*, 31.

28. Henrich, *The Secret of Our Success*, ch. 7.

29. Legare and Souza, "Searching for control."

30. Frazer, *The Golden Bough*.

31. Ibid., 49.

32. Ibid.

33. Mauss, *A General Theory of Magic* (originally *Esquisse d'une théorie générale de la magie*, co-written with Henri Hubert in 1902–1903).

34. Mauss, *A General Theory of Magic*, 176.

35. Carnap, Hahn, and Neurath, "The scientific conception of the world," 306.

36. Ibid., 317.

37. Neurath, "Empirical sociology," 321.

38. Ibid., 320 (italics in original).

39. Ibid., 321.

40. For example, Copenhaver, *Magic in Western Culture*.

41. Bruno, *Cause, Principle and Unity, and Essays on Magic*, 36.

42. Yates, *Giordano Bruno and the Hermetic Tradition*.

43. Hanegraaff, "Beyond the Yates paradigm."

44. Waddell, *Magic, Science, and Religion*.

45. Whyte, "The roots of the silver tree."

46. Bruno, *Cause, Principle and Unity, and Essays on Magic*, 105.

47. Somerville, *On the Connexion of the Physical Sciences*.

48. Whewell, "*On the Connexion of the Physical Sciences*, by Mrs. Somerville."

49. Bruno, *Cause, Principle and Unity, and Essays on Magic*, 105.

50. Vermeir, "Wonder, magic, and natural philosophy," 44–45.

Chapter 5

1. McClenon and Nooney, "Anomalous experiences reported by field anthropologists."

2. Sperber, *Explaining Culture*.

3. White, *An Introduction to the Cognitive Science of Religion*.

4. Smith, "Religion, religions, religious."

5. Boyer, *Religion Explained*; McCauley, *Why Religion is Natural*.

6. Purzycki and Sosis, *Religion Evolving*.

7. Sosis and Bressler, "Cooperation and commune longevity."

8. See, e.g., De Cruz and De Smedt, *A Natural History of Natural Theology*.

9. See chapter 3 for a more detailed conceptual exploration of what cognitive technologies are.

10. Asma, *Why We Need Religion*.

11. Purzycki and Sosis, *Religion Evolving*.

12. Xunzi, *Xunzi, the Complete Text*.

13. Gibson, *The Ecological Approach to Visual Perception*; Romdenh-Romluc, "Habit and attention."

14. Merleau-Ponty, *Phenomenology of Perception*, 129.

15. Romdenh-Romluc, "Habit and attention," 13.

16. Rietveld, "Affordances and unreflective freedom."

17. Luhrmann, *When God Talks Back*, 39.

18. Luhrmann, "A hyperreal God and modern belief."

19. Merleau-Ponty, *Sense and Non-Sense*, 177–78.

20. Ibid., 178.

21. Ibid., 172.

22. Merleau-Ponty, *Phenomenology of Perception*, x. Not all phenomenologists were unsympathetic to Descartes. For example, Edmund Husserl, *Cartesian Meditations*, saw Descartes's *Meditations* as formative for phenomenology.

23. Merleau-Ponty, *Phenomenology of Perception*, xiv–xv.

24. Ibid., xv.

25. Ibid.

26. Williams, "Maurice Merleau-Ponty and the philosophy of religion," 650.

27. See, e.g., Cuneo, *Ritualized Faith*; De Cruz, "Etiological challenges to religious practices."

28. Williams, "Maurice Merleau-Ponty and the philosophy of religion," 650.

29. Descartes, "Passions of the soul," 53, CSM 1:350.

30. The idea that our philosophical and scientific concepts are always provisional and need to be updated is a common theme among American pragmatists. We see this, for instance, in William James's concept of truth as expounded in James, *Pragmatism, and Four Essays from "The Meaning of Truth"*, or Jane Addams's concept of ethics in *Democracy and Social Ethics*.

31. Heschel, *God in Search of Man*, 3.

32. In several passages, Heschel adheres to a non-cognitivist theory of emotions. He denies that awe and wonder are emotions, or at least that they are mere emotions; for example, he writes that awe is "more than an emotion" (*God in Search of Man*, 74). His account of awe and wonder does fit a cognitivist account of emotions which I accept (but will not defend here), and hence I term Heschelian awe and wonder "emotions," even though Heschel himself does not.

33. Heschel, *God in Search of Man*, 46.

34. Wettstein, *The Significance of Religious Experience*.

35. Heschel, *God in Search of Man*, 91.

36. Ibid., 112 (italics in original).

37. Alston, *Perceiving God*.

38. Teresa of Ávila, *The Interior Castle*.

39. Ibn Tufayl, *Hayy Ibn Yaqzān*.

40. Weger and Wagemann, "Towards a conceptual clarification of awe and wonder," 1387.

41. Ibid., 1392.

42. Ibid.

43. Know-how is important to make sure the building does not collapse under its own weight, as happened in the late Middle Ages during the building of some cathedrals, such as Beauvais Cathedral, which collapsed twice and remains unfinished to this day. Hagia Sophia still shows state-of-the-art technological solutions in the way the roof is built to protect it against the earthquakes that frequently occur in Turkey.

44. Joye and Verpooten, "An exploration of the functions."

45. Tiwald and Van Norden, "The gateless barrier," 110 (my parentheses).

46. Ibid.

47. Chung, "Moral cultivation."

48. Carter, *The Japanese Arts and Self-Cultivation*, 59–60.

49. Whitehouse, *Modes of Religiosity.*

50. White, "Personal acts, habit, and embodied agency."

51. Seligman et al., *Ritual and Its Consequences*, 104.

Chapter 6

1. Shmatov and Stephan, "Advances in ball lightning research."

2. Daston and Park, *Wonders and the Order of Nature.*

3. Schuyl, *A Catalogue of All the Cheifest Rarities.*

4. Interview with Hester Loeff, conducted May 31, 2022. For examples of her work, see Hesters Rariteitenkabinet, https://hesterloeff.nl/.

5. Westrum, "Science and social intelligence about anomalies."

6. Waddell, *Magic, Science, and Religion.*

7. Bynum, "Wonder."

8. Perry and Ritchie, "Magnets, magic, and other anomalies."

9. Augustine, "The usefulness of belief."

10. Daston and Park, *Wonders and the Order of Nature*, 237.

11. Henry, *Knowledge is Power.*

12. Fransen, "Weapon salve in the Renaissance."

13. Poskett, *Horizons.*

14. The original Nahuatl version is lost, but the Latin translation, *Libellus de medicinalibus indorum herbis*, survives and can be freely consulted online (https://commons.wikimedia.org/wiki/File:Libellus de Medicinalibus Indorum Herbis.pdf).

15. Poskett, *Horizons*, 123–24.

16. Rockwood, "Descartes on necessity and the laws of nature."

17. De Cruz and De Smedt, *A Natural History of Natural Theology*, ch. 8.

18. Hume, *An Enquiry concerning Human Understanding*, § 10, "Of miracles."

19. Steinhart, *Believing in Dawkins.*

20. Dawkins, *Unweaving the Rainbow*, 39; Keats, *Lamia*, 60.

21. Dawkins, *Unweaving the Rainbow*, 17.

22. Dawkins, "Is science a religion?," 27.

23. Deane-Drummond, "Experiencing wonder and seeking wisdom," 587.

24. Feynman, Layton, and Sands, *The Feynman Lectures on Physics*, vol. 1: *Mainly Mechanics*, 3–11, footnote.

25. Carlson, "Appreciation and the natural environment."

26. Dawkins, *Unweaving the Rainbow*, 6–7.

27. Minet et al., "A new taxonomic status for Darwin's 'predicted' pollinator."

28. This and the next two sections are expanded and modified versions of a short piece I published in *Aeon* magazine: De Cruz, "The necessity of awe." Reproduced with permission of *Aeon*.

29. Kuhn, *The Structure of Scientific Revolutions*.

30. Wegener, "Die Entstehung der Kontinente."

31. Pellegrini, "Styles of thought on the continental drift debate."

32. See Irving, "The role of latitude in mobilism debates," for a review.

33. Van Fraassen, *The Empirical Stance*, 102.

34. Kitcher, "The division of cognitive labor."

35. Van Fraassen, *The Empirical Stance*.

36. Sartre, *Sketch for a Theory of the Emotions*.

37. Ibid., 63.

38. Solomon, *Dark Feelings, Grim Thoughts*, 101.

39. The *Sketch* also contains an account of the emotion of horror, which appears to be in tension with the magical transformation theory offered for joy, anger, and fear. A reconciliation between the two accounts is offered by Andreas Elpidorou, "Horror, fear, and the Sartrean account of emotions."

40. James, "What is an emotion?"; James, *The Principles of Psychology*.

41. Valdesolo, Shtulman, and Baron, "Science is awe-some"; Cuzzolino, "'The awe is in the process.'"

42. Kant, "Universal natural history."

43. Ibid., 1:254, 220.

44. Ibid., 1:255, 221.

45. Ibid., 1:368, 307.

46. Darwin, *On the Origin of Species*, 491.

47. Stellar, "Awe helps us remember."

48. Morton, "Epistemic emotions."

49. Gottlieb, Keltner, and Lombrozo, "Awe as a scientific emotion."

50. McPhetres, "Oh, the things you don't know."

51. Cuzzolino, "'The awe is in the process.'"

52. Ibid., 691.

53. Ibid., 693.

54. Heschel, *God in Search of Man*, 46.

55. Shea, "Imitation as an inheritance system," 2434.

56. Cuzzolino, "'The awe is in the process,'" 692.

57. Gross, *The Scientific Sublime*.

58. Cuzzolino, "'The awe is in the process,'" 691 (italics in original).

59. Burke, *A Philosophical Enquiry*, 138.

60. Bradley, "Darwin's sublime."

61. Darwin, *On the Origin of Species*, 285.

62. Somerville, *On the Connexion of the Physical Sciences*, 311–12.

63. Heschel, *Man Is Not Alone*, 78.

Chapter 7

1. Le Guin, *A Wizard of Earthsea*, 19–20.

2. Nussbaum, *The Frontiers of Justice*, 94.

3. Bendik-Keymer, "The reasonableness of wonder."

4. Bergland, "The power of awe."

5. Reynolds, "An 'awe-walk' might do wonders."

6. Robson, "The little earthquake that could free your mind."

7. Kaplan, "Self-care as self-blame redux."

8. Usher, Durkin, and Bhullar, "Eco-anxiety."

9. Albrecht, "Chronic environmental change."

10. Jaquelyn Gill, https://twitter.com/JacquelynGill/status/1465762764828254210, November 30, 2021 (retrieved June 26, 2023).

11. Note that DDT is still permitted, as an exemption, for use in places with malaria. Also, Carson did not argue that no pesticides should be used. Rather, she advocated the use of more integrated, biologically sustainable methods instead of the indiscriminate dousing of the environment with pesticides that was the practice at the time. I will not delve into the controversy here, but see, e.g., EPA, "DDT—A brief history and status."

12. Gross, *The Scientific Sublime*.

13. Carson, *Silent Spring*, 2.

14. Ibid.

15. Sideris, "Fact and fiction, fear and wonder."

16. Gross, *The Scientific Sublime*, 149.

17. Carson, cited in Moore, "The truth of the barnacles," 266.

18. The original title of the article was "Help your child to wonder."

19. Carson, *The Sense of Wonder*, 15.

20. Ibid., 44.

21. Ibid., 98.

22. Carson, *Lost Woods,* 163.

23. Moore, "The truth of the barnacles."

24. Ibid., 267.

25. Lombardo, *Bhagavad Gita.*

26. Paul, *Transformative Experience.*

27. Pettigrew, *Choosing for Changing Selves.*

28. Carel and Kidd, "Expanding transformative experience."

29. Ibid., 203.

30. Ahmed, *The Cultural Politics of Emotion.*

31. Ibid., 179.

32. Ibid.

33. Flanagan, *The Geography of Morals.*

34. Nussbaum, "Transitional anger."

35. Cherry, *The Case for Rage.*

36. Lorde, "The uses of anger."

37. Ward, "Feeling, knowledge, self-preservation."

38. Cherry, *The Case for Rage,* 25.

39. Ahmed, *The Cultural Politics of Emotion.*

40. Heschel, *God in Search of Man.*

41. Carson, *The Sense of Wonder.*

42. McDowell, *Mind, Value, and Reality.*

43. Vigani, "Beyond silencing."

44. Chen and Mongrain, "Awe and the interconnected self."

Chapter 8

1. Percy, *The Moviegoer,* 18.

2. Ibid.

3. Storm, *The Myth of Disenchantment.*

4. Falchi et al., "The new world atlas of artificial night sky brightness."

5. Williams, *Stand Out of Our Light,* 9.

6. Táíwò, *Elite Capture.*

7. Le Guin's acceptance speech can be viewed online at https://www.youtube.com/watch?v=Et9Nf-rsALk.

8. Descartes, "Passions of the soul," CSM 1:353.

9. Merleau-Ponty, *Phenomenology of Perception,* xv.

10. James, "Remarks on Spencer's definition of mind, 7.

REFERENCES

Addams, J., *Democracy and Social Ethics*. London: MacMillan, 1902
Agrippa, H. C., *Three Books of Occult Philosophy* [1533], trans. E. Purdue. Rochester, VT: Inner Traditions, 2021
Ahmed, S., *The Cultural Politics of Emotion* (2nd edn). Edinburgh: Edinburgh University Press, 2014
Albrecht, G., "Chronic environmental change: Emerging 'psychoterratic' syndromes," in I. Weissbecker (ed.), *Climate Change and Human Well-Being*, pp. 43–56. Dordrecht: Springer, 2011
Algoe, S. B. and J. Haidt, "Witnessing excellence in action: The 'other-praising' emotions of elevation, gratitude, and admiration." *Journal of Positive Psychology*, 4.2 (2009): 105–27
Alston, W. P., *Perceiving God: The Epistemology of Religious Experience*. Ithaca, NY: Cornell University Press, 1991
Alves, R. R., I. L.Rosa, and G. G. Santana, "The role of animal-derived remedies as complementary medicine in Brazil." *BioScience*, 57.11 (2007): 949–55
André, Y. M., *La Vie du R. P. Malebranche* [1888]. Paris: Ingold, 1970
Arango-Muñoz, S. and K. Michaelian, "Epistemic feelings, epistemic emotions." *Philosophical Inquiries*, 2.1 (2014): 97–122
Aristotle, *Metaphysics* [4th c. BCE], trans. C.D.C. Reeve. Indianapolis: Hackett, 2016
Asma, S., *Why We Need Religion*. New York: Oxford University Press, 2018
Augustine of Hippo, "The usefulness of belief" (*De utilitate credenda* [5th c. CE]), in J.H.S. Burleigh (ed.), *Augustine: Earlier Writings*, pp. 284–323. Philadelphia: Westminster Press, 1953
Bai, Y., L. A. Maruskin, S. Chen, A. M. Gordon, J. E. Stellar, G. D. McNeil, K. Peng, and D. Keltner, "Awe, the diminished self, and collective engagement: Universals and cultural variations in the small self." *Journal of Personality and Social Psychology*, 113.2 (2017): 185–209
Barrett, L. F., "Are emotions natural kinds?" *Perspectives on Psychological Science*, 1.1 (2006): 28–58
Beagle, P. S., *The Last Unicorn*. New York: Viking, 1968

Bendik-Keymer, J. D., "The reasonableness of wonder." *Journal of Human Development and Capabilities*, 18.3 (2017): 337–55

Berger, S., *The Art of Philosophy: Visual Thinking in Europe from the Late Renaissance to the Early Enlightenment*. Princeton, NJ: Princeton University Press, 2017

Bergland, C., "The power of awe: A sense of wonder promotes loving-kindness," *Psychology Today*, May 20, 2015, https://www.psychologytoday.com/us/blog/the-athletes-way/201505/the-power-awe-sense-wonder-promotes-loving-kindness (accessed June 26, 2023)

Blanchette, I. and A. Richards, "The influence of affect on higher level cognition: A review of research on interpretation, judgement, decision making and reasoning." *Cognition and Emotion*, 24.4 (2010): 561–95

Boyer, P., *Religion Explained: The Evolutionary Origins of Religious Thought*. London: Vintage, 2002

Bradley, B. S., "Darwin's sublime: The contest between reason and imagination in *On the Origin of Species*." *Journal of the History of Biology*, 44.2 (2011): 205–32

Brassfield, S., "Never let the passions be your guide: Descartes and the role of the passions." *British Journal for the History of Philosophy*, 20.3 (2012): 459–77

Brown, D., *Descartes and the Passionate Mind*. Cambridge: Cambridge University Press, 2006

Brown, D. E., *Human Universals*. New York: McGraw-Hill, 1991

Bruno, G., *Cause, Principle and Unity* [1584], *and Essays on Magic* [1588], ed. and trans. R. de Lucca [*Cause, Principle*] and R. Blackwell [*Essays*]). Cambridge: Cambridge University Press, 2012

Burke, E., *A Philosophical Enquiry into the Origin of Our Ideas of the Sublime and Beautiful* [1757], ed. P. Guyer. Oxford: Oxford University Press, 2015

Bynum, C. W., "Wonder." *American Historical Review*, 102.1 (1997): 1–26

Carel, H. and I. J. Kidd, "Expanding transformative experience." *European Journal of Philosophy*, 28.1 (2020): 199–213

Carlson, A., "Appreciation and the natural environment." *Journal of Aesthetics and Art Criticism*, 37.3 (1979): 267–75

Carnap, R., H. Hahn, and O. Neurath, "The scientific conception of the world: The Vienna Circle" [1929], in M. Neurath and R. S. Cohen (eds), *Empiricism and Sociology*, pp. 299–318. Dordrecht: Reidel, 1973

Carson, R., *The Edge of the Sea*. Boston, MA: Houghton Mifflin, 1955

Carson, R., "Help your child to wonder." *Woman's Home Companion*, July 1956, pp. 24–48

Carson, R., *Lost Woods: The Discovered Writing of Rachel Carson*. Boston, MA: Beacon Press, 1999

Carson, R., *The Sea around Us*. Oxford: Oxford University Press, 1951

Carson, R., *The Sense of Wonder*. New York: Harper and Row, 1965

Carson, R., *Silent Spring* [1962], 50th anniversary edn. Boston, MA: Harper and Row, 2012

Carson, R., *Under the Sea Wind: A Naturalist's Picture of Ocean Life*. New York: Simon and Schuster, 1941

Carter, R. E., *The Japanese Arts and Self-Cultivation*. Albany, NY: State University of New York Press, 2008

Cavanagh, P., "The artist as neuroscientist." *Nature*, 434 (2005): 301–7

Chen, S. K. and M. Mongrain, "Awe and the interconnected self." *Journal of Positive Psychology*, 16.6 (2021): 770–78

Cherry, M., *The Case for Rage: Why Anger is Essential to Anti-racist Struggle*. Oxford: Oxford University Press, 2021

Chung, J. "Moral cultivation: Japanese gardens, personal ideals, and ecological citizenship." *Journal of Aesthetics and Art Criticism*, 76.4 (2018): 507–18

Clark, A. and D. Chalmers, "The extended mind." *Analysis*, 58: 7–19

Clewis, R. R., "Why the sublime is aesthetic awe." *Journal of Aesthetics and Art Criticism*, 79.3 (2021), 301–14

Clore, G. L. and J. R. Huntsinger, "How emotions inform judgment and regulate thought." *Trends in Cognitive Sciences*, 11.9 (2007): 393–99

Clute, J. and J. Grant (eds), *The Encyclopedia of Fantasy*. New York: Houghton Mifflin Harcourt, 1997

Cochrane, T., "The emotional experience of the sublime." *Canadian Journal of Philosophy*, 42.2 (2012): 125–48

Cochrane, T., *The Emotional Mind: A Control Theory of Affective States*. Cambridge: Cambridge University Press, 2018

Copenhaver, B. P., *Magic in Western Culture: From Antiquity to the Enlightenment*. Cambridge: Cambridge University Press, 2015

Cuneo, T., *Ritualized Faith: Essays on the Philosophy of Liturgy*. Oxford: Oxford University Press, 2016

Cuzzolino, M. P., "'The awe is in the process': The nature and impact of professional scientists' experiences of awe." *Science Education*, 105.4 (2021): 681–706

Damasio, A. R., *Descartes' Error: Emotion, Reason and the Human Brain*. New York: Avon, 1994

Danvers, A. F., M. J. O'Neil, and M. N. Shiota, "The mind of the 'happy warrior': Eudaimonia, awe, and the search for meaning in life," in J. Vittersø (ed.), *Handbook of Eudaimonic Well-Being*, pp. 323–35. Dordrecht: Springer, 2016

Danvers, A. F. and M. N. Shiota, "Going off script: Effects of awe on memory for script-typical and -irrelevant narrative detail." *Emotion*, 17.6 (2017): 938–52

Darbor, K. E., H. C. Lench, W. E. Davis, and J. A. Hicks, "Experiencing versus contemplating: Language use during descriptions of awe and wonder." *Cognition and Emotion*, 30.6 (2016): 1188–96

Darwin, C., *The Descent of Man, and Selection in Relation to Sex*, vol. 1. London: John Murray, 1871

Darwin, C., *The Expression of the Emotions in Man and Animals*. London: John Murray, 1872

Darwin, C., *On the Origin of Species by Means of Natural Selection or the Preservation of Favoured Races in the Struggle for Life*. London: John Murray, 1859

Daston, L. and K. Park, *Wonders and the Order of Nature, 1150–1750*. New York: Zone Books, 1998

Dawkins, R., "Is science a religion?" *The Humanist*, 57 (1997): 26–39

Dawkins, R., *Unweaving the Rainbow: Science, Delusion and the Appetite for Wonder*. Boston, MA: Houghton Mifflin, 1998

Deane-Drummond, C., "Experiencing wonder and seeking wisdom." *Zygon: Journal of Religion and Science*, 42.3 (2007): 587–90

De Cruz, H., "Etiological challenges to religious practices." *American Philosophical Quarterly*, 55.4 (2018): 329–40

De Cruz, H., "The necessity of awe." *Aeon*, July 10, 2020, https://aeon.co/essays/how-awe-drives-scientists-to-make-a-leap-into-the-unknown (accessed June 26, 2023)

De Cruz, H. (ed.), *Philosophy Illustrated*. Oxford: Oxford University Press, 2022

De Cruz, H. and J. De Smedt, *A Natural History of Natural Theology: The Cognitive Science of Theology and Philosophy of Religion*. Cambridge, MA: MIT Press, 2015

Dennett, D. C., *Breaking the Spell: Religion as a Natural Phenomenon*. Oxford: Allen Lane, 2006

Deonna, J. A. and K. R. Scherer, "The case of the disappearing intentional object: Constraints on a definition of emotion." *Emotion Review*, 2.1 (2010): 44–52

Descartes, R., *Meditations on First Philosophy with Selections from the Objections and Replies* [1641], trans. J. Cottingham. Cambridge: Cambridge University Press, 1996

Descartes, R., "The Passions of the Soul" [1649], in J. Cottingham, R. Stoothoff, and D. Murdoch (eds and trans.), *The Philosophical Writings of Descartes* [CSM], vol. 1, pp. 325–404. Cambridge: Cambridge University Press, 1985

Descartes, R., "The World, or Treatise on light" [ca. 1630], in J. Cottingham, R. Stoothoff, and D. Murdoch (eds and trans.), *The Philosophical Writings of Descartes* [CSM], vol. 1, pp. 79–98. Cambridge: Cambridge University Press, 1985

De Smedt, J. and H. De Cruz, "The role of material culture in human time representation: Calendrical systems as extensions of mental time travel." *Adaptive Behavior*, 19 (2011): 63–76

De Smedt, J. and H. De Cruz , "Toward an integrative approach of cognitive neuroscientific and evolutionary psychological studies of art." *Evolutionary Psychology*, 8.4 (2010): 695–719

Ekman, P., "Basic emotions," in T. Dalgleish and M. Power (eds), *Handbook of Cognition and Emotion*, pp. 45–60. Hoboken, NJ: John Wiley & Sons, 1999

Ekman, P., E. R. Sorenson, and W. V. Friesen, "Pan-cultural elements in facial displays of emotion." *Science*, 164.3875 (1969): 86–88

Elpidorou, A., "Horror, fear, and the Sartrean account of emotions." *Southern Journal of Philosophy*, 54.2 (2016): 209–25

EPA [United States Environmental Protection Agency], "DDT—A brief history and status," https://www.epa.gov/ingredients-used-pesticide-products/ddt-brief-history-and-status (accessed June 26, 2023)

Falchi, F., P. Cinzano, D. Duriscoe, C. C. Kyba, C. D. Elvidge, K. Baugh, B. A. Portnov, N. A. Rybnikova, and R. Furgoni, "The new world atlas of artificial night sky brightness." *Science Advances*, 2.6, https://www.science.org/doi/10.1126/sciadv.1600377

Feynman, R., R. B. Layton, and M. Sands, *The Feynman Lectures on Physics* [1963], vol. 1: *Mainly Mechanics, Radiation, and Heat*. New York: Basic Books, 2010

Flanagan, O., *The Geography of Morals: Varieties of Moral Possibility*. Oxford: Oxford University Press, 2017

Fontenelle, B. de, *Conversations on the Plurality of Worlds* [1686], trans. H. Hargreaves. Berkeley, CA: University of California Press, 1990

Fransen, S., "Weapon salve in the Renaissance," in M. Sgarbi (ed.), *Encyclopedia of Renaissance Philosophy*, pp. 1–3. Cham: Springer, 2018

Frazer, J., *The Golden Bough: A Study in Magic and Religion* [1922]. Basingstoke: Palgrave MacMillan, 1990

Frijda, N. H., *The Emotions*. Cambridge: Cambridge University Press, 1986

Garcia-Pelegrin, E., A. K. Schnell, C. Wilkins, and N. S. Clayton, "Exploring the perceptual inabilities of Eurasian jays (*Garrulus glandarius*) using magic effects." *Proceedings of the National Academy of Sciences USA*, 118.24 (2021), https://doi.org/10.1073/pnas.2026106118

Gibson, J. J., *The Ecological Approach to Visual Perception*. Boston, MA: Houghton Mifflin, 1979

Girten, K. M., "'Sublime luxuries' of the Gothic edifice: Immersive aesthetics and Kantian freedom in the novels of Ann Radcliffe." *Eighteenth-Century Fiction*, 28.4 (2016): 713–38

Gladwin, T., *East is a Big Bird: Navigation and Logic on Puluwat Atoll*. Cambridge, MA: Harvard University Press, 1970

Godfrey-Smith, P., *Metazoa: Animal Life and the Birth of the Mind*. New York: Farrar, Straus, and Giroux, 2020

Gordon, A. M., J. E. Stellar, C. L. Anderson, G. D. McNeil, D. Loew, and D. Keltner, "The dark side of the sublime: Distinguishing a threat-based variant of awe." *Journal of Personality and Social Psychology*, 113.2 (2017): 310–28

Goto-Jones, C., *Conjuring Asia: Magic, Orientalism, and the Making of the Modern World*. Cambridge: Cambridge University Press, 2016

Gottlieb, S., D. Keltner, and T. Lombrozo, "Awe as a scientific emotion." *Cognitive Science*, 42 (2018): 2081–94

Greenberg, S., "Descartes on the passions: Function, representation, and motivation." *Noûs*, 41.4 (2007): 714–34

Griffiths, P. and A. Scarantino, "Emotions in the wild," in P. Robbins and M. Aydede (eds), *The Cambridge Handbook of Situated Cognition*, pp. 437–53. Cambridge: Cambridge University Press, 2009

Griskevicius, V., M. N. Shiota, and S. L. Neufeld, "Influence of different positive emotions on persuasion processing: A functional evolutionary approach." *Emotion*, 10.2 (2010): 190–206

Gross, A. G., *The Scientific Sublime: Popular Science Unravels the Mysteries of the Universe*. New York: Oxford University Press, 2018

Hadot, P., *Philosophy as a Way of Life: Spiritual Exercises from Socrates to Foucault* [1981], ed. A. I. Davidson, trans. M. Chase. Oxford: Blackwell, 1995

Hammond, N., "Pascal's *Pensées* and the art of persuasion," in N. Hammond (ed.), *The Cambridge Companion to Pascal*, pp. 235–52. Cambridge: Cambridge University Press, 2006

Hanegraaff, W. J., "Beyond the Yates paradigm: The study of Western esotericism between counterculture and new complexity." *Aries*, 1.1 (2001): 5–37

Hass, L., "Life magic and staged magic: A hidden intertwining," in F. Coppa, L. Hass, and J. Peck (eds), *Performing Magic on the Western Stage from the Eighteenth Century to the Present*, pp. 13–31. Basingstoke: Palgrave MacMillan, 2008

Henrich, J., *The Secret of Our Success: How Culture is Driving Human Evolution, Domesticating Our Species, and Making Us Smarter*. Princeton, NJ: Princeton University Press, 2018

Henry, J., *Knowledge is Power: How Magic, the Government and an Apocalyptic Vision Inspired Francis Bacon to Create Modern Science*. London: Icon Books, 2002

Heschel, A. J., *God in Search of Man: A Philosophy of Judaism* [1955]. London: Souvenir, 2009

Heschel, A. J., *Man Is Not Alone: A Philosophy of Religion*. New York: Farrar, Straus and Giroux, 1951

Hesters Rariteitenkabinet (Hester Loeff), https://hesterloeff.nl/ (accessed June 26, 2023)

Heyes, C. M., *Cognitive Gadgets: The Cultural Evolution of Thinking*. Cambridge, MA: Harvard University Press, 2018

Hooke, R., *Micrographia, or Some Physiological Descriptions of Minute Bodies Made by Magnifying Glasses; with Observations and Inquiries Thereupon*. London: The Royal Society, 1665

Hume, D., *An Enquiry concerning Human Understanding* [1748], ed. P. Millican. Oxford: Oxford University Press, 2007

Hume, D., "The natural history of religion" [1757], in T. L. Beauchamp (ed.), *A Dissertation on the Passions. The Natural History of Religion. A Critical Edition*, pp. 30–87. Oxford: Clarendon Press, 2007

Husserl, E., *Cartesian Meditations: An Introduction to Phenomenology* [1929], trans. D. Cairns. Dordrecht: Springer, 1977

Hutchins, E., "The cultural ecosystem of human cognition." *Philosophical Psychology*, 27.1 (2014): 34–49

Ibn Tufayl, *Hayy Ibn Yaqzān: A Philosophical Tale* [12th c. CE], ed. and trans. L. E. Goodman. Chicago: University of Chicago Press, 2003

Irving, E., "The role of latitude in mobilism debates." *Proceedings of the National Academy of Sciences USA*, 102 (2005): 1821–28

James, W., *Pragmatism* [1907], *and Four Essays from "The Meaning of Truth"* [1909]. New York: Meridian Books, 1955

James, W., *The Principles of Psychology*. New York: Henry Holt and Co., 1890

James, W., "Remarks on Spencer's definition of mind as correspondence." *Journal of Speculative Philosophy*, 12.1 (1878): 1–18

James, W., "What is an emotion?" *Mind*, 9.34 (1884): 188–205

Jastrow, J., "Psychological notes upon sleight-of-hand experts." *Science*, 3.71 (1896): 685–89

Joye, Y. and J. Verpooten, "An exploration of the functions of religious monumental architecture from a Darwinian perspective." *Review of General Psychology*, 17 (2013), 53–68

Kant, I., *Critique of Practical Reason* [1788], trans. W. Pluhar. Cambridge: Hackett, 2002

Kant, I., "Observations on the feeling of the beautiful and sublime" [1764], in Kant, *"Observations on the Feeling of the Beautiful and Sublime" and Other Writings*, ed and trans. P. Frierson and P. Guyer, pp. 13–202. Cambridge: Cambridge University Press, 2011

Kant, I., "Universal natural history and theory of the heavens, or Essay on the constitution and the mechanical origin of the whole universe according to Newtonian principles" [1755], trans. O. Reinhardt, in Kant, *Natural Science*, ed. E. Watkins, pp. 182–308. Cambridge: Cambridge University Press, 2012

Kaplan, J., "Self-care as self-blame redux: Stress as personal and political." *Kennedy Institute of Ethics Journal*, 29.2 (2019): 97–123

Keats, J., *Lamia* [1820]. Philadelphia: J. B. Lippincott, 1888

Keltner, D., *Awe: The New Science of Everyday Wonder and How It Can Transform Your Life*. New York: Penguin, 2023

Keltner, D. and J. Haidt, "Approaching awe, a moral, spiritual, and aesthetic emotion." *Cognition and Emotion*, 17 (2003): 297–314

Keltner, D. and J. Haidt, "Social functions of emotions at four levels of analysis." *Cognition and Emotion*, 13.5 (1999): 505–21

Keltner, D. and P. K. Piff, "Self-transcendent awe as a moral grounding of wisdom." *Psychological Inquiry*, 31.2 (2020): 160–63

Keltner, D., D. Sauter, J. Tracy, and A. Cowen, "Emotional expression: Advances in basic emotion theory." *Journal of Nonverbal Behavior*, 43.2 (2019): 133–60

Kim, K., "Adam Smith's *History of Astronomy* and view of science." *Cambridge Journal of Economics*, 36.4 (2012): 799–820

Kirkham, N. and C. Letheby, "Psychedelics and environmental virtues." *Philosophical Psychology*, March 29, 2022, https://doi.org/10.1080/09515089.2022.2057290

Kitcher, P., "The division of cognitive labor." *Journal of Philosophy*, 87 (1990): 5–22

Koelsch, S., A. M. Jacobs, W. Menninghaus, K. Liebal, G. Klann-Delius, C. Von Scheve, and G. Gebauer, "The quartet theory of human emotions: An integrative and neurofunctional model." *Physics of Life Reviews*, 13 (2015): 1–27

Krueger, J., "Affordances and the musically extended mind." *Frontiers in Psychology*, 4, art. 1003 (January 2014), https://doi.org/10.3389/fpsyg.2013.01003

Kuhn, G., A. Pailhès, and Y. Lan, "Forcing you to experience wonder: Unconsciously biasing people's choice through strategic physical positioning." *Consciousness and Cognition*, 80 (April 2020), https://doi.org/10.1016/j.concog.2020.102902

Kuhn, T. S., *The Structure of Scientific Revolutions*. Chicago: Chicago University Press, 1962

Lamont, P., "A particular kind of wonder: The experience of magic past and present." *Review of General Psychology*, 21.1 (2017): 1–8

Legare, C. H. and M. Nielsen, "Ritual explained: Interdisciplinary answers to Tinbergen's four questions." *Philosophical Transactions of the Royal Society B*, 375.1805 (June 2020), https://doi.org/10.1098/rstb.2019.0419

Legare, C. H. and A. L. Souza, "Evaluating ritual efficacy: Evidence from the supernatural." *Cognition*, 124.1 (2012): 1–15

Legare, C. H. and A. L. Souza, "Searching for control: Priming randomness increases the evaluation of ritual efficacy." *Cognitive Science*, 38.1 (2014): 152–61

Le Guin, U. K., acceptance speech, The National Book Foundation's Medal for Distinguished Contribution to American Letters, 65th National Book Awards, November 19, 2014, https://www.youtube.com/watch?v=Et9Nf-rsALk (accessed June 26, 2023)

Le Guin, U. K., *A Wizard of Earthsea* [1968]. Boston, MA: Houghton Mifflin, 2012

Levy, M. and F. Mendlesohn, *Children's Fantasy Literature: An Introduction*. Cambridge: Cambridge University Press, 2016

Lewontin, R. C., "The organism as the subject and object of evolution." *Scientia*, 118 (1983): 65–82

Libellus de medicinalibus indorum herbis, available at https://commons.wikimedia.org/wiki/File:Libellus de Medicinalibus Indorum Herbis.pdf (accessed June 26, 2023)

Lomas, T., "Towards a positive cross-cultural lexicography: Enriching our emotional landscape through 216 'untranslatable' words pertaining to well-being." *Journal of Positive Psychology*, 11.5 (2016): 546–58

Lombardo, S., *Bhagavad Gita: A New Verse Translation*. Indianapolis: Hackett, 2019

Lorde, A., "The uses of anger." *Women's Studies Quarterly*, 25.1/2 (1997): 278–85

Luhrmann, T. M., "A hyperreal God and modern belief: Toward an anthropological theory of mind." *Current Anthropology*, 53.4 (2012): 371–95

Luhrmann, T. M., *When God Talks Back: Understanding the American Evangelical Relationship with God*. New York: Vintage, 2012

Malinowski, B., *Magic, Science, and Religion, and Other Essays* [1925]. Prospect Heights, IL: Waveland Press, 1992

Masuda, T., P. C. Ellsworth, B. Mesquita, J. Leu, S. Tanida, and E. van de Veerdonk, "Placing the face in context: Cultural differences in the perception of facial emotion." *Journal of Personality and Social Psychology*, 94.3 (2008): 365–81

Mauss, M., *A General Theory of Magic*, trans. R. Brain [1950]. London: Routledge, 2001

McCauley, R. N., *Why Religion Is Natural and Science Is Not*. Oxford: Oxford University Press, 2011

McClenon, J. and J. Nooney, "Anomalous experiences reported by field anthropologists: Evaluating theories regarding religion." *Anthropology of Consciousness*, 13 (2002): 46–60

McDowell, J., *Mind, Value, and Reality*. Cambridge, MA: Harvard University Press, 1998

McPhetres, J., "Oh, the things you don't know: Awe promotes awareness of knowledge gaps and science interest." *Cognition and Emotion*, 33.8 (2019): 1599–615

Merleau-Ponty, M. *Phenomenology of Perception* [1945], trans. C. Smith. London: Routledge, 2002

Merleau-Ponty, M., *Sense and Non-Sense* [1945–1947], trans. H. L. Dreyfus and P. A. Dreyfus. Evanston, IL: Northwestern University Press, 1964

Minet, J., P. Basquin, J. Haxaire, D. C. Lees, and R. Rougerie, "A new taxonomic status for Darwin's 'predicted' pollinator: *Xanthopan praedicta* stat. nov." *Antenor*, 8.1 (2021): 69–86

Moore, K. D., "The truth of the barnacles: Rachel Carson and the moral significance of wonder." *Environmental Ethics*, 27.3 (2005): 265–77

Morton, A., "Epistemic emotions," in P. Goldie (ed.), *The Oxford Handbook of Philosophy of Emotion*, pp. 385–99. Oxford: Oxford University Press, 2020

Most, G., "Philosophy begins in wonder," in A. te Heesen, M. Fend, C. von Oertzen, and F. Vidal (eds), *Surprise: 107 Variations on the Unexpected*, pp. 289–91. Berlin: Max Planck Institute for the History of Science, 2019

NASA, "NASA's Webb delivers deepest infrared image of universe yet," July 12, 2022, https://www.nasa.gov/image-feature/goddard/2022/nasa-s-webb-delivers-deepest-infrared-image-of-universe-yet (accessed June 26, 2023)

Nesse, R. M., "Evolutionary explanations of emotions." *Human Nature*, 1.3 (1990): 261–89

Neurath, O., "Empirical sociology: The scientific content of history and political economy" [1931], in O. Neurath, *Empiricism and Sociology*, ed. M. Neurath and R. S. Cohen, pp. 319–440. Dordrecht: Reidel, 1973

Nussbaum, M., *The Frontiers of Justice: Disability, Nationality, Species Membership*. Cambridge, MA: Harvard University Press, 2006

Nussbaum, M., "Transitional anger." *Journal of the American Philosophical Association*, 1.1 (2015): 41–56

Oliver, M. B., "Tender affective states as predictors of entertainment preference." *Journal of Communication*, 58.1 (2008): 40–61

Pailhès, A. and G. Kuhn, "Influencing choices with conversational primes: How a magic trick unconsciously influences card choices." *Proceedings of the National Academy of Sciences USA*, 117.30 (2020): 17675–79

Parris, B. A., G. Kuhn, G. A. Mizon, A. Benattayallah, and T. L. Hodgson, "Imaging the impossible: An fMRI study of impossible causal relationships in magic tricks." *Neuroimage*, 45.3 (2009): 1033–39

Pascal, B., *Pensées* [1670], ed. and trans. R. Ariew. Indianapolis: Hackett 2004

Paul, L. A., *Transformative Experience*. Oxford: Oxford University Press, 2014

Peirce, C. S., "The fixation of belief," *Popular Science Monthly*, 12 (November 1877): 1–15

Pellegrini, P. A., "Styles of thought on the continental drift debate." *Journal for General Philosophy of Science*, 50.1 (2019): 85–102

Percy, W., *The Moviegoer*. New York: Avon Books, 1961

Perry, J. and S. L. Ritchie, "Magnets, magic, and other anomalies: In defense of methodological naturalism." *Zygon: Journal of Religion and Science*, 53.4 (2018): 1064–93

Pettigrew, R., *Choosing for Changing Selves*. Oxford: Oxford University Press, 2020

Piff, P. K., P. Dietze, M. Feinberg, D. M. Stancato, and D. Keltner, "Awe, the small self, and prosocial behavior." *Journal of Personality and Social Psychology*, 108.6 (2015), 883–99

Pinker, S., *How the Mind Works*. London: Allen Lane, 1997

Plato, *"Theaetetus" and "Sophist"* [4th c. BCE], ed. and trans. C. Rowe. Cambridge University Press: Cambridge, 2015

Pober, J., "What emotions really are (in the theory of constructed emotions)." *Philosophy of Science*, 85.4 (2018): 640–59

Porubanova, M., D. J. Shaw, R. McKay, and D. Xygalatas, "Memory for expectation-violating concepts: The effects of agents and cultural familiarity." *PLoS One*, 9.4 (2014), https://doi.org/10.1371/journal.pone.0090684

Poskett, J., *Horizons: A Global History of Science*. London: Penguin, 2022

Potts, R., *Humanity's Descent: The Consequences of Ecological Instability*. New York: Avon Books, 1996

Prinz, J., "How wonder works," *Aeon*, June 21, 2013, https://aeon.co/essays/why-wonder-is-the-most-human-of-all-emotions (accessed June 24, 2023)

Purzycki, B. G. and R. Sosis, *Religion Evolving: Cultural, Cognitive, and Ecological Dynamics*. Sheffield: Equinox, 2002

Rensink, R. A. and G. Kuhn, "A framework for using magic to study the mind." *Frontiers in Psychology*, 5, art. 1508 (February 2015), https://doi.org/10.3389/fpsyg.2014.01508

Reynolds, G., "An 'awe-walk' might do wonders for your well-being," *The New York Times*, September 30, updated October 1, 2020, https://www.nytimes.com/2020/09/30/well/move/an-awe-walk-might-do-wonders-for-your-well-being.html (accessed June 26, 2023)

Richerson, P. J. and R. Boyd, *Not by Genes Alone: How Culture Transformed Human Evolution*. Chicago: University of Chicago Press, 2005

Rietveld, E., "Affordances and unreflective freedom," in R. T. Jensen and D. Moran (eds), *The Phenomenology of Embodied Subjectivity*, pp. 21–42. Dordrecht: Springer, 2013

Rietveld, E., "Situated normativity: The normative aspect of embodied cognition in unreflective action." *Mind*, 117.468 (2008): 973–1001

Robson, D., "The little earthquake that could free your mind," BBC Worklife, January 6, 2022, https://www.bbc.com/worklife/article/20220103-awe-the-little-earthquake-that-could-free-your-mind (accessed 24 June 2023)

Rockwood, N., "Descartes on necessity and the laws of nature." *Journal of Analytic Theology*, 10 (2022): 277–92

Rolfe, C., "Theatrical magic and the agenda to enchant the world." *Social and Cultural Geography*, 17.4 (2016): 574–96

Romdenh-Romluc, K., "Habit and attention," in R. T. Jensen and D. Moran (eds), *The Phenomenology of Embodied Subjectivity*, pp. 3–19. Dordrecht: Springer, 2013

Russell, J. A., "Culture and the categorization of emotions." *Psychological Bulletin*, 110.3 (1991): 426–50

Sanderson, B., *The Hero of Ages* (Book 3 of *Mistborn*). New York: Tor Books, 2009

Sanderson, B., "Sanderson's First Law," newsletter, February 20, 2007, https://www.brandonsanderson.com/sandersons-first-law/ (accessed June 24, 2023)

Sartre, J.-P., *Sketch for a Theory of the Emotions* [1939], trans. P. Mairet. London: Methuen, 1962

Schliesser, E., *Adam Smith: Systematic Philosopher and Public Thinker*. Oxford: Oxford University Press, 2017

Schliesser, E., "Wonder in the face of scientific revolutions: Adam Smith on Newton's 'proof' of Copernicanism." *British Journal for the History of Philosophy*, 13 (2005): 697–732

Schuyl, F., *A Catalogue of All the Cheifest [sic] Rarities in the Publick Anatomie-Hall of the University of Leyden* [1695]. Leiden: Diewertje vander Boxe, 1723

Seligman, A., R. P. Weller, M. J. Puett, and B. Simon, *Ritual and Its Consequences: An Essay on the Limits of Sincerity*. Oxford: Oxford University Press, 2008

Seneca, "On sophistical argumentation" (Epistle 45) [ca. 62–65 CE], in [Lucius Annaeus] Seneca, *Epistles*, vol. 1: *Epistles 1–65* [LCL 75], trans. R. M. Gummere, pp. 290–97. Cambridge, MA: Harvard University Press, 1917

Seth, A., *Being You: A New Science of Consciousness*. New York: Dutton, 2021

Shea, N., "Imitation as an inheritance system." *Philosophical Transactions of the Royal Society of London B: Biological Sciences*, 364 (2009): 2429–43

Shiota, M. N., "Awe, wonder, and the human mind." *Annals of the New York Academy of Sciences*, 1501.1 (2021): 85–89

Shiota, M. N., D. Keltner, and A. Mossman, "The nature of awe: Elicitors, appraisals, and effects on self-concept." *Cognition and Emotion*, 21 (2007): 944–63

Shmatov, M. L. and K. D. Stephan, "Advances in ball lightning research." *Journal of Atmospheric and Solar-Terrestrial Physics*, 195 (2019), https://doi.org/10.1016/j.jastp.2019.105115

Sideris, L. H., "Fact and fiction, fear and wonder: The legacy of Rachel Carson." *Soundings*, 91.3/4 (2008): 335–69

Smail, D. L., *On Deep History and the Brain*. Berkeley, CA: University of California Press, 2008

Smith, A., "The history of astronomy," in A. Smith, *Essays on Philosophical Subjects*, ed. J. Black and J. Hutton, pp. 1–130. Dublin: Wogan, Byrne, Moore et al., 1795

Smith, A., *An Inquiry into the Nature and Causes of the Wealth of Nations*. London: W. Strahan and T. Cadell, 1776

Smith, A., *The Theory of Moral Sentiments*. Edinburgh: Andrew Millar, Alexander Kincaid and J. Bell, 1759

Smith, J. Z., "Religion, religions, religious," in M. C. Taylor (ed.), *Critical Terms for Religious Studies*, pp. 269–84. Chicago: University of Chicago Press, 1998

Solomon, R. C., *Dark Feelings, Grim Thoughts: Experience and Reflection in Camus and Sartre*. Oxford: Oxford University Press, 2006

Somerville, M., *On the Connexion of the Physical Sciences*. London: John Murray, 1834

Sosis, R. and E. R. Bressler, "Cooperation and commune longevity: A test of the costly signaling theory of religion." *Cross-Cultural Research*, 37 (2003): 211–39

Spencer, H., *The Principles of Psychology*. London: Longman, Brown, Green, and Longmans, 1855

Sperber, D., *Explaining Culture: A Naturalistic Approach*. Oxford: Blackwell, 1996

Spinoza, B. de, "Ethics demonstrated in geometric order" [1677], in Spinoza, *The Collected Works of Spinoza*, ed. and trans. E. Curley, vol. 1, pp. 408–617. Princeton, NJ: Princeton University Press, 1985

Spinoza, B. de, "Short treatise on God, man, and his well-being" [ca. 1661], in Spinoza, *The Collected Works of Spinoza*, ed. and trans. E. Curley, vol. 1, pp. 53–156. Princeton, NJ: Princeton University Press, 1985

Steinhart, E., *Believing in Dawkins: The New Spiritual Atheism*. Cham: Springer, 2020

Stellar, J. E., "Awe helps us remember why it is important to forget the self." *Annals of the New York Academy of Sciences*, 1501.1 (2021): 81–84

Stellar, J. E., A. M. Gordon, P. K. Piff, D. Cordaro, C. L. Anderson, Y. Bai, L. A. Maruskin, and D. Keltner, "Self-transcendent emotions and their social functions: Compassion, gratitude, and awe bind us to others through prosociality." *Emotion Review*, 9.3 (2017): 200–207

Stephan, A., S. Walter, and W. Wilutzky, "Emotions beyond brain and body." *Philosophical Psychology*, 27.1 (2014): 65–81

Storm, J. A., *The Myth of Disenchantment: Magic, Modernity, and the Birth of the Human Science*. Chicago: University of Chicago Press, 2017

Táíwò, O. O., *Elite Capture. How the Powerful Took Over Identity Politics (and Everything Else)*. Chicago: Haymarket Books, 2002

Teller, "What Is Magic?" (MasterClass, Arts and Entertainment: *Penn & Teller Teach the Art of Magic*, lecture 4), https://www.masterclass.com/classes/penn-and-teller-teach-the-art-of-magic/chapters/what-is-magic (accessed June 26, 2023)

Teresa of Ávila. *The Interior Castle, or The Mansions* [1577], ed. B. Zimmerman. London: Thomas Baker, 1921

Thomson, A. L. and J. T. Siegel, "Elevation: A review of scholarship on a moral and other-praising emotion." *Journal of Positive Psychology*, 12.6 (2017): 628–38

Tiwald, J. and B. Van Norden, "The gateless barrier," trans. S. Addiss, in J. Tiwald and B. Van Norden (eds), *Readings in Later Chinese Philosophy: Han Dynasty to the 20th Century*, pp. 110–12. Indianapolis: Hackett, 2014

Tolkien, J.R.R., *The Lord of the Rings*. London: Allen & Unwin, 1954–1955

Tracy, J. L. and D. Randles, "Four models of basic emotions: A review of Ekman and Cordaro, Izard, Levenson, and Panksepp and Watt." *Emotion Review*, 3.4 (2011): 397–405

Tversky, A. and D. Kahneman, "Judgment under uncertainty." *Science*, 185 (1974): 1124–31

Usher, K., J. Durkin, and N. Bhullar, "Eco-anxiety: How thinking about climate change-related environmental decline is affecting our mental health." *International Journal of Mental Health Nursing*, 28 (2019): 1233–34

Valdesolo, P., A. Shtulman, and A. S. Baron, "Science is awe-some: The emotional antecedents of science learning." *Emotion Review*, 9.3 (2017): 215–21

Van Fraassen, B. C., *The Empirical Stance*. New Haven, CT: Yale University Press, 2002

Van Norden, B. W., *Taking Back Philosophy: A Multicultural Manifesto*. New York: Columbia University Press, 2017

Vermeir, K., "Wonder, magic, and natural philosophy: The disenchantment thesis revisited," in M. F. Deckard and P. Losonczi (eds), *Philosophy Begins in Wonder. An Introduction to Early Modern Philosophy, Theology, and Science*, pp. 43–71. Cambridge: James Clarke, 2011

Vigani, D., "Beyond silencing: Virtue, subjective construal, and reasoning practically." *Australasian Journal of Philosophy*, 99.4 (2021): 748–60

Vivaldo, G., E. Masi, C. Taiti, G. Caldarelli, and S. Mancuso, "The network of plants volatile organic compounds." *Scientific Reports*, 7.1 (2017): 1–18

Waddell, M., *Magic, Science, and Religion in Early Modern Europe*. Cambridge: Cambridge University Press, 2021

Ward, C., "Feeling, knowledge, self-preservation: Audre Lorde's oppositional agency and some implications for ethics." *Journal of the American Philosophical Association*, 6.4 (2020): 463–82

Wegener, A., "Die Entstehung der Kontinente." *Geologische Rundschau*, 3 (1912): 276–92

Weger, U. and J. Wagemann, "Towards a conceptual clarification of awe and wonder." *Current Psychology*, 40.3 (2021): 1386–1401

Westrum, R., "Science and social intelligence about anomalies: The case of meteorites." *Social Studies of Science*, 8.4 (1978): 461–93

Wettstein, H., *The Significance of Religious Experience*. Oxford: Oxford University Press, 2012

Whewell, W., "*On the Connexion of the Physical Sciences*, by Mrs. Somerville." *The Quarterly Review*, 51 (1834): 54–68

White, C., *An Introduction to the Cognitive Science of Religion: Connecting Evolution, Brain, Cognition and Culture*. London: Routledge, 2021

White, J., "Personal acts, habit, and embodied agency in Merleau-Ponty's *Phenomenology of Perception*," in J. Dunham and K. Romdenh-Romluc (eds), *Habit and the History of Philosophy*, pp. 152–65. Abingdon: Routledge, 2023

White, L. A., *The Evolution of Culture: The Development of Civilization to the Fall of Rome* [1959]. Walnut Creek, CA: Left Coast Press, 2007

Whitehouse, H., *Modes of Religiosity: A Cognitive Theory of Religious Transmission*. Walnut Creek, CA: AltaMira Press, 2004

Whyte, J., "The roots of the silver tree: Boyle, alchemy, and teleology." *Studies in History and Philosophy of Science, Part A*, 85 (2021): 185–91

Williams, J., "Maurice Merleau-Ponty and the philosophy of religion." *Religious Studies*, 57.4 (2021): 634–53

Williams, J., *Stand Out of Our Light: Freedom and Resistance in the Attention Economy*. Cambridge: Cambridge University Press, 2018

Xunzi, *Xunzi, the Complete Text* [3rd c. BCE], trans. E. L. Hutton. Indianapolis: Hackett, 2016

Yates, F., *Giordano Bruno and the Hermetic Tradition*. Chicago: University of Chicago Press, 1964

Zhuangzi [attr.], *Zhuangzi*, ed. and trans. H. Höchsmann and Y. Guorong. Abingdon: Routledge, 2006

Zuckert, R., "Awe or envy: Herder contra Kant on the sublime." *Journal of Aesthetics and Art Criticism*, 61.3 (2003): 217–32

Zurn, P., "Wonder and *écriture*: Descartes and Irigaray, writing at intervals," in M. Rawlinson (ed.), *Engaging the World: Thinking after Irigaray*, pp. 115–34. Albany, NY: State University of New York Press, 2016

INDEX

A NOTE ON THE TYPE

This book has been composed in Arno, an Old-style serif typeface in the classic Venetian tradition, designed by Robert Slimbach at Adobe.